All There Is

Also by Tony Parsons:

The Open Secret

Nothing Being Everything

This Freedom

All There Is

Tony Parsons

First published in Great Britain 2003
Revised 2012

© Tony Parsons 2003, 2012, 2020
All rights reserved

Cover from a series of paintings
'Inner Landscapes' by John Miller

Text in Palatino

Published by Open Secret Publishing
For contact details, please visit
www.theopensecret.com

A catalogue record for this book is available
from the British Library

ISBN 978-0-9533032-2-9

Contents

This book is dedicated to Claire.

Love beyond the speaking of it

All there is is this ... and that ...

being

the one appearing as two
nothing appearing as everything
the absolute appearing as the relative
emptiness appearing as fullness
the uncaused appearing as the caused
unicity appearing as separation
subject appearing as object
the singular appearing as plurality
the impersonal appearing as the personal
the unknown appearing as the known

It is silence sounding and stillness moving and these
words appearing as pointers to the wordless

... and yet nothing is happening

Foreword

The Sanskrit word Advaita points to that which cannot be spoken of and exposes the utter futility of the idea that something called a seeker could discover something else called enlightenment. This work embraces and describes this revolutionary perception that brings with it the realisation that what had been sought had never been lost.

Here is the final piece of a puzzle that never was.

There are apparently many so-called spiritual teachers, gurus and enlightened masters, and the main thrust of their message is based on the presumption that there is such a thing as a separate individual who is capable of making choices and generating effort in order to become worthy of attaining something called enlightenment. This kind of teaching is rooted in a deep ignorance about the nature of liberation, and it continuously reinforces the idea of seeking and becoming.

But oneness does not emerge through something gained, but rather through something lost …

When the apparent separate identity falls away, the radiant wonder of being becomes apparent – to no one. It also becomes clear that there was no one who ever needed to be liberated.

This theme runs continuously through this work, but if you dip into the book rather than plod through it, page by page, looking for 'the answer', you could begin to sense a flavour of something that is beyond answers.

Discussions take place firstly at the level of the exchange of concepts, within which context it is possible that confused ideas about our original nature can be displaced by a clarity that is both uncompromising and mysterious. At another level, what is being shared in silence is already known. Wisdom speaks to wisdom, nothing speaks to nothing, and it is recognised that we are meeting and resonating with that which already is.

Tony Parsons   *May 2003*

London
October 2002

I'd better warn you right away that I'm not an enlightened person and no person in this room will ever become enlightened. There is no such thing as an enlightened person. It's a contradiction in terms.

All that's happening here, really, is that we are friends together, remembering something. This is just about remembering something that maybe we feel we have lost or mislaid. Some people here have remembered – also, quite a lot of people in this room have sensed or glimpsed what they thought was lost.

And the nature of what we think is lost is timeless being. It's totally, utterly simple – the one thing we long for more than anything else is actually totally and utterly simple and immediate and available. And strangely enough, the thing that we long for has never left us.

In simple terms, all that happens is that when we are very young children, there is simply being, without a knowing of being; there is simply being. And then someone comes along and says 'You're Bill' or 'You're Mary' – 'You're a person'. And in some way or other, the mind – the 'I' thought, the identity, the idea that 'I am a person' – takes over the energy of being and identifies it as Bill or Mary or whatever. It takes over being and gives it a name. Words begin, labels begin, and the whole idea of 'me' becomes the main investment of living.

If you look at the apparent world we live in today, it's all about 'me' – it's all about 'the person' being successful or being a failure. We grow up believing and reinforcing the idea that there

1

is someone, and that that someone lives a life that's going to last so many years. We're in a journey called 'my life', and the thing to do – we are told – is to make that life work. The whole investment is in 'I am a person and I've got to make my life work'.

And so you get lists fed to you. The first one is about being a good child, the next one is about being a good student … Then there's a list of requirements about being a good worker, usually followed by being a good husband, wife or partner. Some people turn to religion to try to discover what it is that's missing in their lives, and again they are presented with a list of requirements they need to fulfil before they can become worthy or acceptable.

There are as many ideas about how to make your life work as there are apparent people in the world. And there are many subtle levels of personal achievement – some of them apparently negative. For some people, achieving victimhood can seem like a great success!

We have to play that game because we really think we are people; there's a pretence taken on called 'I am a person'. You pretend you are this person, and you take it so seriously that you forget you are pretending – the pretence becomes everything. And many many people live the whole of their lives like that. That's fine, that's divine, that's the divine game.

Some people feel that, having gone through all of these lists, there's still something missing. They then think, 'Maybe I can find it through therapy – maybe a therapist can tell me what's wrong, what's missing'. And they're into another list. And again there is this drive to become something.

But for some reason or other, none of the things on the lists religion, therapy, whatever – seem to work. And then some people hear about something called enlightenment, and they get a sense that maybe that's the last piece of the jigsaw. So they go and find someone who's pretending to be a guru, and they pretend to be disciples. And the two build each other up. The master who will teach you how to become enlightened gets bigger and bigger, and you feel more and more important because your master seems more and more important.

Of course it's yet another wonderful game of pretence. And another list comes with that scenario – meditation, or being very honest, or being so serious about enlightenment you could throw yourself off a cliff ... One of the items on that list is 'being here now' – being here now and not thinking. You can read the books and go and see these guys who tell you this ... And you can actually be here now for up to three or four minutes – and maybe not think for five seconds!

It's all pretence, and it's totally divine. Every moment of your lives up until this moment has been absolutely perfectly divine; nothing could have ever been any different. The whole appearance of your life – the whole of the apparent doing, the apparent choosing – is totally appropriate and divine.

But the idea of 'you' is being reinforced all the time. The emphasis is that there is someone there; everything in the world goes on emphasising that there is someone there. The pretence of 'me' goes on being reinforced even in the search for enlightenment, because what a so-called master will say to you is, 'I have become enlightened – I am an enlightened person and *you* can become an enlightened person'. You – this pretend 'you'! It's a total, utter fallacy, because awakening is the realisation that there is no one – it's as simple as that. It's totally and utterly simple, and also very difficult.

Awakening is the realisation that all that's been happening – the whole idea of there being a 'me' – is a pretence. You're actually pretending to sit there and look at me. You're pretending that you're sitting there looking at me and trying to get something.

Actually, there is no one sitting there and there is nothing to get.

You can close your eyes, if you want to, and sense the energy that you think is 'you'. It's like an aliveness ... For some people it's a sense 'I exist' ...

But that energy, that sense of 'you' being there, is actually not you. That sense of who you think you are – that sense of aliveness and energy – is being; it's just being. It never came and it never went away – it's never left you; it's always been there. You thought it was you – it's just pure being. It isn't who you are – it's what you are. What you are is simply being, presence, life. You are life, life happening, but it doesn't happen to anyone. Sitting on that chair isn't happening to you – sitting on that chair is what's happening, to no one. There's just being. You are being – you are divine being.

And it's so amazing because wherever you go, there is being. Whatever you apparently do, there is being. Whatever you apparently don't do, there is being. There always has been being, whatever you've apparently done or not done, however unworthy or neurotic or ignorant or selfish you think you are. All of those qualities arise in what you are, which is being. All there is is being. And what arises in that being is the idea that 'you' exist.

So you see, how is it possible that anyone needs to do something for awakening to happen? There is no one – there is only being – so how could anyone do anything? Why should anybody have to become something, when all they are is a pretence? Should they become a better pretence? Awakening has absolutely nothing to do with you. You are just a character in a play. Tony Parsons is simply a set of characteristics – that's what is sitting here, a set of characteristics and a body/mind. But what you are is the being, the stillness, from which that comes. All that's actually sitting there is stillness, beingness – call it what you like.

Awakening is simply the dropping of a fantasy, a pretence, an idea of pretending to be someone. And there's nobody here in this room who can drop that idea. What is going on here is that at one level we're talking and the mind is trying to understand, but at another level, there's a deeper wisdom (which we all know anyway) that's being communicated and resonating and being re-acknowledged.

Once this message is heard, then the 'me' simply drops away. The idea of 'me', the pretence of 'me' is absent and there is what is always there – simply being.

It's as simple as that. It's utterly simple. It's right there – you don't have to go anywhere. You don't even have to understand it – don't for goodness' sake try and understand it! And don't think for a moment that anybody wants you to believe it – it has nothing to do with belief. It can be felt … there's just aliveness. There's life, sitting here.

The mind will want to chatter on about this, and that's absolutely fine. If the mind wants to talk or ask questions, let that happen. What's happening is that the questions get no answers and the mind finds that it can't get anywhere, because *this* already is the case. The mind wants to say 'Yes but …' – and that's divine. No question is silly – if it's in the mind, it needs to come out and be responded to.

But somewhere the mind wants to give up. And in the end, all that it's seeing is that there is just this – life.

If you close your eyes, all you actually find are sensations. One thing is happening at a time – the body sitting in a chair is happening; a breeze coming through the window is happening; the crackling of paper is happening; cars are happening … There's no story. The story that we think is our story is simply a pretence, because always there is only this. The story you've listened to about your life is not going anywhere. Everything that is happening is simply the invitation to see that all there is is this. All the time, life has been saying to you, 'Look – there is simply life. There's no story – there's simply life'.

(Long silence)

So there really is nothing I can do to realise this?

It isn't that there's nothing you can do – it is that there is no one. So if there is no one, there is no choice and no doing. But apparent choice and doing appear in that. You could say you might choose to get up and walk out, or have a cup of tea later on; that is an apparent choice that arises. But there's no one in there who makes that choice. No one chose to come here today – they only appeared to make that choice.

When you use the word 'apparent', it gives the impression that this is an appearance of something.

Yes, it is the one appearing as two. There is only oneness, and you are the oneness appearing as two. This is the two appearing, but actually there is only oneness. And this is the appearance, this is the drama of the search for oneness. This is one playing at being two looking for itself. It's as simple as that.

This appearance that we see – the world and our apparent lives – is not going anywhere and has absolutely no purpose or meaning. It only appears to be important and purposeful and meaningful and on a journey towards somewhere. It's a parable. We live in a parable. The world and our life is a metaphor. And what is actually arising is simply the invitation to see that you are the one. So everything we drink, eat, sit on, breathe is the one inviting us to see that we are that.

Right now, you are totally ensconced in your own invitation. Everything that's happening to your senses and your mind and your thinking right at this moment is simply oneness inviting you to see that you are that. That's all this is about.

So is it the mind that wakes up to see that you are that? Is it the mind that sees it?

No, it is no one who sees it; it is being that sees it.

Your experience at the moment is that there is no one and there is only oneness. What would happen if tomorrow you get Alzheimer's or some sort of disease like that where the whole mind just goes chaotic? You would no longer see.

Yes I would, because seeing has nothing to do with the mind or me. The seeing of oneness comes from nothing. Even what's being communicated here most of the time comes out of nothing. So the seeing comes out of nothing and whatever arises – including Alzheimer's or whatever – simply is what arises.

OK, so you see that there is only one – I see two. My mind is seeing that there is separation – for you, there is no separation.

No.

But there is no difference between you and me. Because if there was, if suddenly you had Alzheimer's, then your perception …

There's no difference; there is only oneness. This is oneness appearing. There's no distance between us, there's no space between us; there is only oneness.

But what wakes up to that?

Oneness. Oneness plays the game of being two asleep looking for oneness. When awakening happens, it is only the dropping away of taking twoness seriously; that's all we're talking about here … This whole thing is as simple as this – all that's in the way of awakening is a false idea. It really is. It's a pretence which you've been conditioned to believe. And when the idea that you are two drops away, there is oneness.

o   o   o

When there is 'Yes!' to the words, is it one recognising one?

Yes, but it isn't something to do with understanding, it is more to do with intuition. It is like a leap, a sudden seeing of something that was already known. 'Oh Yes, I already know this.'

And is it more likely to happen by virtue of our being here?

I think in some ways that what goes on here is that the mind walks in with the intention of getting something and begins to realise that it is getting nothing, because nothing is being given. And so it goes on coming, still with the idea of getting something, and in the end it simply gives up.

You see, this is about a love affair. It's to do with a total intimacy just with the wonder of this. It's like a child on the beach building sandcastles, and there's nothing else that exists but the sand and the sea and the saltiness; that's all there is – there isn't anything else. It's the wonder of that simplicity, the wonder of this, which blows everything about concepts out of the window. It's the timeless wonder of what we are.

So you've only really come here to remember something. And yes, if you keep on coming and remembering, somehow what has been piled on top of that remembering just falls away.

So is it about realising the nothingness?

Yes, in the end, you could use those words. It is the seeing of oneness, and in the end there is no-one seeing oneness. There is no-one here, there's just oneness.

o   o   o

So awakening is not an experience, then?

8

No, awakening is not an experience at all. In my vocabulary, if you talk about experience you're talking about an experiencer. Tony Parsons has experiences, but there is only oneness – which is not an experience. So whatever happens for Tony Parsons whatever's happening right now – arms waving, this voice coming out, it's slightly warm in here, coughing's happening – that is simply the manifestation of oneness. And so is Tony Parsons, believe it or not!

So who is it that experiences it as a manifestation of oneness?

No one – it is a mystery. Oh, Tony Parsons experiences heat in the body and whatever. Tony Parsons experiences that, but there is oneness in which all of that appears to happen. I am the one, I am all that is – and so are you. But when I say 'I am', it's got nothing to do with Tony Parsons. Nothing at all. Tony Parsons is just an appearance; he's just a character in the play, meaning nothing – 'All the world's a stage …'

Is that all right? Are you all right with that?

I can't understand it.

No, no. What we're talking about here is totally beyond comprehension; it's utterly beyond comprehension. But there are people sitting in this room who know that there's something watching them sitting in this room. There's something watching you sitting in this room.

*So, can I invite you to close your eyes and tell me immediately – without thinking about it – what arises in your awareness? What do you see or feel?

I feel hot.

So who is it that feels hot?

---

* *The dialogue between the asterisks on this page and the next encapsulates a sequence that occurs frequently at meetings.*

I do.

And where is the 'I' that feels hot?

In my head, thinking it.

And that is just the reporting of information about feeling hot.

Yes.

So already you are the reporter of a story.

Yes, I suppose I am telling you I feel hot.

How about just saying, 'The body feels hot'?

Yes, OK – the body feels hot.

What is it that sees that?

(Long silence)

Something that recognises it.

What is that something like?

It's like a sort of knowing.

And what is the sense that arises out of the simple seeing of what is?

It feels more spacious ... like a timelessness.*

When separation takes place, the 'I' thought comes along and, like a cuckoo bird, lands in the nest and sits on what is. From then on, 'me' thinks that it is the entirety of the universe, and everything that arises is apparently seen from 'me'.

So when we see a tree, we think 'me' is seeing a tree over there, whereas the tree is arising as what is.

That which you have always thought of as 'me' is, in reality, what is.

It never went away but was only misidentified.

This is the one and only constant, and everything else is transient – including the cuckoo bird.

○ ○ ○

So awakening is not necessarily the dropping away of the body/mind or the dropping away of the doer.

Not at all. Well, the apparent doer.

It's not an experience because oneness is always there.

It isn't that oneness is always there – there is actually only oneness. And Tony Parsons isn't possible except in oneness. Because all this is is oneness appearing as two, and Tony Parsons is part of that appearance.

So it's not that that bit of oneness knows there is oneness …

There's no bit of oneness – there is only oneness.

So when Morag says that she doesn't understand, what's that?

That is the mind trying to understand something that's totally beyond the mind.

Is that not in oneness?

Absolutely – that is not understanding arising in oneness.

Right.

Which has been going on – I notice – for quite a long time! The mind can't comprehend oneness, because the oneness, if you like, uses the mind to split everything into two.

This is one *(pointing to wall)*, wall-ing, and it uses the mind as a tool to split this into two, so that it appears in the manifestation, and appears to the seeker to be separate, because the seeker is looking for oneness and in the essence of oneness is the wall, which the seeker thinks is separate from him. In fact, that is the lover, the oneness, inviting the seeker to see that it isn't separate. The wall is the invitation, and sitting on the seat is the invitation; and drinking water and reading a book … all of it is just the one saying, 'There's only oneness'.

The one is trying to communicate with what – itself?

Yes. Don't forget that the one appears to play the game of two and take it seriously. One has become totally two, it seems. It believes totally that it is an individual in a separate world, just for the drama of that all dropping away and seeing one.

I see, so there's a purpose behind this …

You could say that there's a meaning or an essence in everything – the essence of unconditional love is all there is. And it invites the one who longs for unconditional love to discover that all there actually is is unconditional love. You don't have to go anywhere to find it – that's what is.

But you see, it does sound a little bit loopy …

Oh totally!

Because the one is inviting itself to understand …

Forget it – the mind will never comprehend.

The other thing I find a little troublesome is the fact that you are saying it's pointless. Is that correct? Did you use the word 'pointless'?

There's no purpose to this manifestation, no.

But would you say there was a purpose to your talking?

No, no.

So what you're saying is purposeless.

And you've paid good money for it! The words just won't get it. The words and that book and those tapes are not it and never ever will be it.

Yes, so what is the point? I mean, is it important to be here?

Well, there's nothing you can do about it anyway, because there's no one who can choose to be here or not be here. It's not a question of it being important. And it's interesting, after all the seeking, that you're sitting here hearing that you never ever needed to seek. Because somewhere – and there's no question about this – there's a readiness now to hear that, to hear the message totally and utterly directly, totally uncluttered. And you're here hearing it.

o   o   o

This purposelessness the mind is finding troublesome. Are you saying the totality is purposeless?

Yes. It's not going anywhere – in my terms, purpose has a direction towards somewhere; there's a purpose for this or that which leads you somewhere. What I'm saying is there isn't anywhere to go.

Ah, well that's slightly different, because for me, I find it much more acceptable to say, 'The purpose is this, or here, or now …'

You could say life is its own purpose, in a way.

Yes. But to say that it's purposeless or meaningless or pointless is somehow … doesn't sound quite right.

What I'm trying to say is that it's not going anywhere, because in the end what I'm trying to say is *you* don't have to go anywhere. You see, the great difficulty people have with, let's call it enlightenment, is that they've been conditioned to think they've got to go somewhere or become something for that to happen. And what's being said directly now is that that isn't the case. It's got absolutely nothing to do with you at all, or you going anywhere or anything happening to you in that way.

What you are is totally the divine expression. Exactly as you are is it. Exactly as you are is simply the divine expression. So it doesn't have to change – nothing has to change. All that happens in awakening is a totally different perception.

But when you say 'exactly as you are', you don't mean this limited thing sitting on a chair here talking to you?

Is the divine expression. Everything is the divine expression. And what you are is that which sees that.

There are no edges to this divine expression – it runs into everything else?

Well, within the manifestation there seem to be limitations. You can't run a hundred yards in under nine seconds – or can you? You know what I mean. You live in limitation, apparently – that's the fun of the manifestation, that's the fun of the drama. The apparent 'you' lives in limitation. But what you are is all that is. What you are holds all of that in love. What you are isn't a part – what you are is the whole. What you are is the source. You are the source of this appearance.

o   o   o

If oneness is all there is, if this chunk of oneness thinks it's separate from the rest of the one, what difference does it make if this chunk of oneness experiences oneness or not?

No difference.

So why talk about it?

Why not? It's to do with the longing inside – you know, what led you here? There's nothing you can do about it anyway, but some sense that something is missing, or a longing for something that can't be put together in words, brings people to ask the question 'What am I?' or 'Who am I?' (which, incidentally, is the wrong question). People ask, 'Who am I? What is this about?'

The seeing of that is magnificent. It's amazing, it's stunning; it's just absolutely stunning. It's what you're here for, to see that all there is is oneness.

Whose longing is it?

It's the longing that arises in manifestation; it's the longing of the apparent individual who thinks they have lost paradise intentionally, in a way, in order to re-gain it. That's all it is. But the paradise isn't over there – this is it. All there is is this.

So it's a part of paradise that's not in a sense a paradise.

That's how it appears.

Why?

It's just what apparently happens. You can't do anything about it now, and asking 'Why?' is not going to get you anywhere. Asking why is pointless. Just give up asking why and simply see that all there is is this.

Can any question lead us to oneness?

No. Neither can any answer. Nothing can lead you to oneness because there already is only oneness. You can never be led and you can never move towards oneness because it already is.

But we're not aware of that.

Well, you think you aren't; you only think you aren't. The only difference really in this room is that most people own something. 'It's more difficult for a rich man to enter the kingdom of heaven ...' People who come here, seekers, own something. What they own is the idea that there is someone there; what they own is the 'me', the apparent separate identity ... which is a mirage.

o   o   o

How did this happen for you, Tony?

It didn't happen for me.

How did it happen?

It just happened ... I don't know, there's no way of saying how it happened.

Was it anything you did?

No, there's no one there to do anything. Nobody ever did anything. Nobody's actually ever done anything, because there is no one. There are only the appearances of people doing things. That's the game.

You were saying earlier that awakening can happen and the person might think that there's the idea of two again?

Oh yes. Well, what happens is that the two, or the 'me', comes back. But oneness is all there is and what arises in oneness is the sense of 'me'.

What is the difference between true clear vision and an experience?

An experience is something that somebody has, or an apparent person has. Awakening, nobody has. Awakening has nothing to do with experience.

I was reading that Nathan Gill said he had many transcendental experiences. How would I know that for a moment there was clear vision and it was not just a transcendental experience?

There is only one clear seeing that can happen, and when it happens, there's a knowing; there's no question about the nature of that. Afterwards, there is a return to the 'me' – there has to be, to protect the body/mind. There is no such thing as a transcendental

16

experience. There is, however, a transcendental happening and thereafter the perception changes.

OK, there was a recognition that at that moment there was no one but after that the 'me' comes back?

Not necessarily – there can be an immediate establishment in presence. But for most people it's a flip-flop in and out at first. To protect the body/mind there's a flip in, out, in, out. The out gets bigger and bigger and the in gets smaller and smaller.

But there doesn't necessarily have to be any sort of fireworks?

Oh no, that's just a conditioned idea about enlightenment.

o   o   o

This thing about purposelessness – I think I've been trying to find a purpose because I won't accept perfection.

You won't accept perfection?

No, because I'm stuck on the idea that things need fixing. But in fact if it's perfect, it doesn't need a purpose; that which needs a purpose can't be perfect. The difference between you and me is that you see the perfection – I don't.

Yes, there is just total perfection, though I'm not all that keen on the word 'perfection'.

But I still think things need fixing.

All right, but all the time you do, there'll always be something that needs fixing. That's what seeking is. Seeking is always looking for that which already is, but it thinks it can find it over there, or in there, or when something's happened here; it's always next week. Realisation or awakening is the seeing that it already is – there's nothing to find or fix. This is simply an expression of unconditional love.

o o o

Tony, you say that the only thing that's stopping us seeing this is the idea of separation or twoness …

Or the idea that there's something to find.

To me, an idea is a very flimsy, insubstantial thing. If I think the world is flat and it's explained to me once that it's round, I get it. Why is this idea so persistent?

You've got to look back at your own life and everybody else's and the world we live in and see that that idea is the most strongly conditioned belief in the whole world – 'You *are* an individual, you're in a world of individuals and the only way you'll succeed or fail is to try very hard'. That's the whole message of this manifestation. If you look at the apparent world in which we live, it is almost entirely motivated towards individuality.

Let's be simple about it, and say that the year after you were born and living in pure being and not knowing it, suddenly one day you met this thing you suddenly realised was your mother calling you Philip. That moment of separation is the beginning of fear and the feeling of alienation. From that moment onwards, you always long to find that which you knew in that first year. We long to be children and live in the simple wonder of this as it is.

But that's a hugely powerful conditioning, to play this game of being two.

Just to pursue that a bit, conditioning sounds like it's external but what's my part in that?

There is nothing that's external; there is nothing outside or inside.

No, but you know what I mean – it's from other people or society …

18

But those other people arose in your awareness. The people in this room are only arising in that. I am only arising in that awareness – I'm not over here.

And all the people that you meet in your life are uniquely and exactly the people you need to be with to build up and reinforce that sense of separation. But also they arise for you to discover that separation is unreal. It's a paradox – you live in a world that separates you very powerfully from oneness, in order to discover that there is only oneness.

o   o   o

When one is oneness or has recognised it, is the play still ongoing or is one in that position of the child in the joy and wonder of it?

The play still goes on, but no longer is there any idea that it's going anywhere or has any purpose. It's just the play of manifestation; it's one playing the game of twoness. Whereas before that, there was the journey to find that. That's why it is that when the seeker drops away there's often a lot of laughter that happens – suddenly realising that what you're seeking is already right in front of you, and seeing how you were going all over the place looking for the joy and wonder of that which already is.

This drama apparently involves a lot of suffering at times.

It would seem so; there is suffering, yes.

How come?

Well, because basically all the time there is twoness, then there is suffering. Actually we all live in a subtle sort of desperation; we all live in a longing to find oneness. So actually all there is is suffering. And sometimes it's sort of enjoyable and all right, and some people apparently seem to suffer more than others ... But of course in clear seeing it's seen that no one is suffering. There's no one suffering, because there is no one.

19

But there is suffering?

There is suffering, in the appearance.

You say that oneness doesn't have a purpose. Oneness does not transform itself – it is eternally what it is.

There is only oneness, and purpose can appear to arise out of oneness, simply because everything that manifests is oneness manifesting. So avoidance of oneness manifests ... It doesn't need to transform because it's absolutely immaculate. Oneness is immaculate, and everything that arises out of oneness is absolutely immaculate. It doesn't look it, to the mind, but it's immaculate. Because the whole source of everything is only unconditional love, and obviously it embraces everything, including hatred and anger. Nothing is excluded – all is the absolute.

o   o   o

I was with somebody in the past week who died, on Tuesday morning. In a sense, could you say that there was no one who died and there's no one who'll be reborn – it's just aspects of the one?

Yes. No one was born and nobody died, but the appearance of the body/mind ended. How old was this person?

Eighty-five.

All right, so for eighty-five years the appearance of Bill was there – but it was only an appearance. And all that was was one, or light, you could say. So light is all there is, and in the appearance of eighty-five years (which is actually just meaningless) there was a body/mind that went through that. But at the ceasing of the body/mind, at the point of the end of the mind that maintains this picture, there is only light. So Bill last Tuesday was no more but is already what he always is – the light, or oneness, or the absolute.

But Bill wouldn't know that the second after that – Bill won't be around saying 'I am light'. The idea that somewhere Bill or karma continues after death comes totally out of the mind – it has no relationship to reality at all. The mind longs to go on and on and on forever. It just longs to, so it builds up all sorts of ideas about after death. It loves all that.

So this dream, this play goes on after death? The mind in a way can keep it going, with its experiences after death and ideas of karma and all that?

No, you didn't really listen just now. When that body/mind ceases, then the appearance ceases and there isn't anything but light. In fact, there never was anything but light. At apparent death all personal ideas of karma and suchlike evaporate.

It's like a wave on the ocean. You know, there's a wave going along the ocean that actually believes it's a wave – 'Look, I'm a wave! I'm totally separate. I'm bigger than most other waves, much more important'. That's what we do – that's basically what it is. But actually all it is is the ocean, wave-ing. It's the one, wave-ing.

We are the one, wave-ing, and we think we are separate wavers, very important wavers, and we're going to go to a shore that's got sun on it and beautiful sands, because we are so worthy. And other people think they're waves that are going to go into the Antarctic because they're so awful. But actually we are just the ocean, wave-ing. We are the one appearing to be.

And there is no question that that's leading anywhere or has anything to do with what was before, because there never was a before. There never has been a before and there isn't an after. Always there's only this. Tonight, when you're eating your dinner, there will be only this.

o   o   o

You mentioned earlier that when you found this oneness there was a drifting in and out, so that you re-identified with the old ego, shall we say. Are you now permanently in oneness?

No – there is only oneness.

I'm sure everyone, as you said earlier, has had an experience of oneness, but the draw to twoness is so strong that you find yourself re-entangled. How does one maintain it, in practical terms? How can one stay in the oneness?

One can't, because you are not out there. The whole problem with trying to stay with the oneness is the 'I' trying to stay with oneness. Once the 'I' starts trying to stay with oneness, oneness is not apparent anymore.

Let's put it this way – there is only oneness. In time terms, that is, if you like, totally the permanent state – there is only oneness. And nobody experiences that or owns that. But whatever arises in the manifestation arises in that oneness and is oneness, including the ego of Tony Parsons, the characteristics of Tony Parsons.

What we're talking about here is totally radical as far as the old conditioned idea of enlightenment is concerned. In the old conditioned idea of enlightenment we all wanted to believe, enlightenment happens and there is no character there at all there's just total bliss and utter goodness. It is nonsense born out of the ignorance of the mind. Awakening has nothing to do with goodness or bliss – awakening is the realisation that there is only oneness and twoness arises in that, including Tony Parsons.

I am all there is. There are about a hundred egos in this room and I *am* that, I am *that*. Enlightenment isn't becoming a separate island, a separate thing on its own which looks down on everything else and blesses it or is compassionate about it. Awakening is aliveness. It's a love affair with aliveness. It's about dropping the idea that anybody has a life and realising that all there is is life. You don't have a life – you are life, and in life ego, desire, hatred, love all happen. And I am the one in which that happens. And so are you.

So how does karma fit into this?

It doesn't. It's just another part of the mind's idea of keeping the story going. It's a meaningless appearance. Because the whole idea of something like karma is that things are going somewhere you know, if there's karma, and all the karmas you've had over your past lives, there's some idea that actually there is still a journey and a purpose leading to somewhere. We're not going anywhere – this is it. This has always been it – only this. So what's karma got to do with it?

So even talking about it is just the slippery slope again?

Yes, thinking about anything like that is going back into the wheel of becoming, and awakening has nothing to do with becoming.

○   ○   ○

There do seem to be things that I can do which give me an experience, like the thing you were speaking about earlier where one looks for the self, tries to discover that. Would you say there are actually practices that lead one to a greater awareness of oneness?

No, absolutely not. What I'm suggesting here is that you see it from a totally different point of view. What you're still talking about is a person who has choice. This message is not speaking to a person; it doesn't recognise any people in this room, or any sense of a choice. This is nothing talking to nothing. And nothing is hearing and saying, 'Yeah!' And the mind is saying, 'Oh yeah, but hold on a minute – could I do this or that?' – not seeing the point, that there is no one. It isn't, 'Can you do anything?' – there isn't anyone there. There appears to be – one can appear to go home and walk up into the quiet room at the back and meditate. And for some people, why not? That's what happens. But there is nobody there who is actually making that choice.

You've never made a choice in your life. The choice appears to come in from somewhere, and you think you own it and are acting upon it. You never have – there isn't anyone. Look for the one who makes the choice.

o   o   o

I feel that this is almost too difficult a route to go down, using words, and it just churns me up. I feel like almost being sick with the anxiety of the words, because they're going nowhere.

For you.

For me they're going nowhere. They're getting completely stuck. And I know that that's the wrong route.

It's best not to listen.

My mind just wants to work it all out.

No, no – I should have said right at the beginning, 'Don't listen to anything for the next three hours'! You don't have to.

There are people in this room who don't ever need to hear this – already the seeker has vanished. They come because there's something else going on here that's far more powerful than all these words.

OK, so is that a sensation?

No. *You're* trying to put it into words now!

Because I'm trying to put it into the realm of my own experience.

It has nothing to do with your experience.

That's all I have.

That's all you apparently have, but what is it that sees that experience?

But it feels like it's never going to happen.

No, it isn't going to happen to you – it will never happen to you. It hasn't happened to me. There is no such thing as an enlightened person.

I feel you're playing with the words that I'm speaking.

I'm not. Is it possible you don't really want to hear about something that is totally beyond the mind? The main thing about coming here is to go away with absolutely nothing. As long as you've paid, that's all right! It's the most expensive nothing in town! *(Laughter)*

You're just playing a game here.

No, I'm not, but it is.

You're playing with my ego – you're almost like hitting it against the wall, you're hitting all our egos against the wall.

Yes, absolutely, because the mind is full of crap ideas. The mind wants an answer, but in the end the answer that comes back defeats the mind and it can't get hold of anything. So what happens here – and it's happening more and more and more – is that the mind gives up. And it longs to give up and say, 'I don't get it ... Oh! Ah!'

o   o   o

In the oneness, are there, like, several minds asking lots of questions or is it one mind in the oneness with just oodles of questions and ideas and nonsense and whatever?

There are apparent individuals, and the secret is only found by the apparent individual seeker. So let's say there are a hundred apparent seekers in this room. The individual – the apparent individual, the seeker – has to re-discover the secret himself. That's why no institution holds the secret. Christianity and Buddhism have nothing to do with this. They are simply religious dogmatic movements; they have no connection with awakening at all, simply because awakening is for the individual seeker.

You could say that each question … I must have been asked three hundred times, 'Why is there suffering in the world?' People say to me, 'Don't you get pissed off with that question?' No, because every time it's asked, it comes out of a total uniqueness.

So my sense is that uniquely we are all one looking for the realisation that we are one. We are being that has forgotten we are being. It's as simple that. We're just trying to remember something that we've mislaid somewhere. That is it. It's totally and utterly simple. But in another way it's colossally difficult, because to find it, we're frightened we'll lose ourselves. And strangely enough, losing ourselves is the finding of it.

o   o   o

Given that the actual wanting of awakening implies an identification that has in the end to be given up, wouldn't it be valid to point out to people that it is in fact more likely to happen through self-enquiry, through a questioning of this sense of identification?

So who is it who will choose to do self-enquiry?

Well, you don't have to tell people to do anything …

No, they just go on apparently doing it anyway. That includes not only self-enquiry but meditation and all kinds of processes of becoming. And yet there are people in this world who no longer look for enlightenment but it happens.

I know that some people never do self-enquiry and it still happens because it happens. But for most people, self-enquiry, looking inwards, does seem to be the way.

It may seem like that for you, and all the time there is an apparent 'you', there can be a strong fascination with the idea of doing something in order to reach somewhere.

But self-enquiry as awareness, not as a doing?

All I can say to that is that everything that is apparently being done through everyone in this room and everywhere else is totally perfect as it is. It's totally appropriate, and it arises in awareness, which is definitely not self-enquiry. That's my point. Because nobody could ever do anything – nobody's ever done anything that hasn't been absolutely perfect, in every way. It could never have been any other way. The whole basis of self-enquiry presumes that there is an individual choice to do something and get somewhere.

Tony, this is a bit pedantic of me but if you ask for a show of hands here, as to who has engaged in some practice, my guess is most hands would go up.

Yes, I would think probably 70%, though quite a lot of people who come here have given that up actually. But so what?

Oh, it just satisfies my pedantic mind.

Would it then make you feel that a practice is better than not? Because if I asked everybody in this room how many of them would like to win the Lottery, then they'd all put up their hands but it wouldn't mean that winning the Lottery would make you happy.

You've lost me there but never mind!

Ask the 70% of people in this room if practice has got them any nearer to awakening.

o   o   o

27

When you just said a minute ago that everything that's happening in the world is unique and perfect, I immediately thought of Hitler. Where's his role in all that, in your view?

Oh, to be Hitler. Hitler was the one arising as Hitler, just as Hussein is the one arising as Hussein. There's no Hitler there there's nobody there being Hitler. Hitler is happening through that body/mind. It's as simple as that.

But in terms of what we are doing here, presumably we've got good motivations for being here …

No, you might think you have, but they're totally selfish! You've come here to find something that you want.

They're totally perfect, of course!

Absolutely perfect, but not good or bad.

On the one hand you're saying our motivations are selfish …

But selfishness is perfect – everything is perfect.

So it's rather a pointless word, isn't it?

Well, in one way, but in answer to the original question, you haven't come here out of goodness – you've come here because you think you wanted to, and because you think you're going to get something. That's what happens; that's what seeking is about. What at the end of the afternoon you may find is that, although you came here to find something or to get something, there's nothing to get.

But sometimes there is.

Oh, well, yes, in the world there are things to get – in the appearance of the world. The mind wants to get things all the time, and that's absolutely perfect.

o   o   o

When I first started to seek, in a conscious way, it was brought to my attention by various teachers that the mind was the problem, if you like; it was obscuring this oneness or peacefulness or whatever. But I was so entrenched in my mind that to simply try and watch … In the end I found I had to use my mind to log what the watching part had seen, if that makes sense. It's like, if I was a computer and I could only understand Fortran, I had to translate everything into Fortran for quite a while, before I could see without decoding, before I could just see it and let it go.

So in a way if we say, 'We don't use our minds', that's just another thought. That's another thing that the mind will say; that's another rule that it's making.

There isn't anything wrong with the mind – I never said there was. The mind is the mind. But when it's seen clearly, it's seen as what it is, as just a collection of thoughts, and it is just as divine as selfishness or goodness.

What I'm saying is that though these days I don't need to use my mind so much, initially, when it was so entrenched, I had to use my mind to lose my mind, to loosen its hold.

Yes, that's what's going on here; that's fine, absolutely fine. But actually, it wasn't you using the mind to lose the mind – that's the problem.

No, it wasn't, and I can see that. Even at the time I could see it, but I knew I had to translate it, I knew I had to log it in to my mind, because that was the only language I understood, that my ego understood.

But you will one day come to the realisation that it wasn't even you doing that logging. There's no one there who chooses to do that logging; it just happens.

○   ○   ○

There are people who say there are certain things you can do that help; that there is an idea called help; that help is a real thing. What does it mean, to help?

29

Well, there's an idea of help and there's also an idea of someone who can choose to help, themselves or other people. Both ideas are rooted in ignorance.

Well, I would say that you're helpful.

Hold on a minute – what's coming out of here has got nothing to do with Tony Parsons. The one is speaking to the one. And you could say, if you still think there is something like help, then that is helping. But actually as far as the one is concerned, you don't need helping because there isn't anyone there to help; and also, what is there is divine. Nobody in this room needs any help. There isn't anybody anyway, but also, this is divine; this is absolutely divine. Who needs help?

But people who are in suffering – my clients who come and they are suffering and I can tell they're suffering, they're in deep pain and I can see they're in deep pain … I find it very difficult sometimes.

But the problem is that you think that *they* are suffering.

Yes, I know.

To see that they aren't can already lift them out of that. That's compassion. And anyway, helping somebody who's suffering doesn't have anything to do with awakening. All you're doing is helping someone who's suffering.

It's like, you could go to therapy and forgive your mother and resolve your problems with your sexuality – all you end up with is a person who's forgiven their mother and resolved their problems with their sexuality. It's got nothing to do with awakening at all. It's like a lot of teachings which talk about the way you should be – you should be honest or serious or meditate or whatever it is. All you end up with is someone who's honest and serious and meditates a lot and eats watercress or whatever. So what?

o   o   o

Returning to the analogy of the one as water and the waves in the ocean, I'm just wondering if the notion of soul – not at an ego level or a mind level but some sort of spirit – is the one.

Although I wasn't a Catholic I went to a Catholic school, and the soul to me is a sort of red thing that looks a bit like a heart; it has a hole in it with blood dripping out. People talk about a soul in new age language, they call it mind/body/spirit. It's an utterly clueless title – as though there's a mind and then there's body and then there's spirituality and they're all in three separate compartments. It's the mind trying to sectionalise. There is just oneness, and everything that manifests, everything that moves, is oneness moving.

There are some teachers who apparently teach 'through the heart' or talk about the heart a lot. But again, it's very confusing because it seems geographical. I know it's not meant to be geographical – it's meant to be about the heart of love and all that. But it's confusing because somehow it pinpoints it into one thing. There is only oneness – end of story.

So with this concept of soul, it's some sort of reference to something which ...

Well, the mind wants to sectionalise so the mind calls a soul something that is spiritual and apart from everything else. That's my sense of what the soul is. The soul is usually used in Catholicism more than anywhere else. Because they've got to create the catechism (which is a horrendous list of things you should and shouldn't do – I always enjoy the mortal sins the most!), they're using that language and they had to find a word which compartmentalises the thing in you which is nearest to God.

OK, supposing we accept this basic idea that you've got ...

You can't! But let's say that you do. Mind you, you wouldn't be asking me any questions if you had.

All right, let me just burble on a bit. There is this oneness – so what? What is that doing?

Nothing at all. However, oneness manifests and appears as doing.

Right. I suppose I've got this underlying idea that this is supposed to resolve a lot of problems.

No, no, you see you're back to the soul, really. Somewhere what you've done in the mind is compartmentalise oneness like some people do presence, as though it's something that's floating around which has a goodness about it, so if we all got in touch with it we'd be better people. This is totally nothing to do with what's being talked about here – nothing at all.

I suppose I'm finding it difficult to get hold of this idea of the pointlessness or the purposelessness of it, because somehow I can't believe that you're standing there without a purpose, and that you've come down here today from Cornwall ... Although you're going to say that you haven't come down here, that somehow you're just here ... You see what I'm trying to say?

Nothing has ever happened. Nothing will ever happen. Nobody will ever go anywhere, because there's nowhere to go this is it. Therefore everything that manifests has the essence of love in it, because it comes from the source of love. And therefore everything that manifests is inviting oneness to be seen by those who can't see it, or apparently those who can't see it. So everything in its essence is love inviting, is the lover inviting.

But it isn't doing something in your life here and then there, to lead you on to somewhere else. It's actually right now shouting out loud to you, and you don't want to listen because you want to find intention; your mind wants to find intention that will move it towards somewhere else. It wants to believe in purpose in order to avoid oneness.

The last thing that the mind wants to do is stop and let there just be the seeing of this. We don't want to do it – we're much more excited about the adventure of enlightenment and all the other adventures that there are and the girl down the road you fancy … The mind doesn't want to know about 'Stop! Let there just be the seeing of this'. The mind can't do that. Let there just be the seeing of this – just standing on the ground, or hearing the car, or laughing … That is what is. That is the beloved. That is love speaking. Car? That's not a car – that's the beloved, saying 'I am the one'.

OK, let's go back to Hitler – is that the beloved?

Oneness is represented in every form. Nothing can be denied because there is only the absolute. Liberation isn't liberation if it doesn't embrace non-liberation. Unconditional love embraces everything; unconditional love is the source of all that is, including the appearance of someone that you've called Hitler, who you think was a separate person who wilfully gassed the Jews. This is oneness – this is immaculate love, believe it or not.

And the other thing that can be realised is that in that appearance is a totally neutral balance. So as Hitler gasses the Jews, there's a balance elsewhere. There's always a total balance; everything is held in balance.

o   o   o

Is it possible to free oneself from the mind by effort?

Who is it that would do that? Who is in there that can choose to free themselves? What you will realise is that awakening is the dropping of the sense of 'me', and the last thing 'me' wants to do is drop. So 'me' can't choose to kill itself.

So how is it brought about? How is awakening brought about?

It isn't brought about; nothing can bring it about. And once it's seen that nothing can bring it about, then there's a letting go. You can't do it, but there's an 'Ah! At last, I realise after all these years of struggle and endeavour to be better or still or drop the ego suddenly I see it's utterly pointless'. There is just this, the seeing of this.

Would you describe that as renunciation?

Well, you could – it's a rather grand word, but yes. It's the dropping of 'me', and no one can do that. But once the seed has been planted, in a way suddenly everything starts to change. People give up the idea that they can get anywhere and something new takes over. It's happening.

o   o   o

A question has been bubbling up in me most of the afternoon. In a few words it is 'Can I know?'

You can't, but what you are knows. When you say 'know', I use the word in the sense of 'seeing', not 'knowledge'. What you are sees what is, and in the end sees itself.

I think my question is coming from the fact that many statements that you've made this afternoon ... I can imagine myself saying them, and I'm projecting myself into imaginary conversations where someone says, 'Where are you getting that from? Surely this is just your mind. You're telling me the mind never gets it so what are you talking from? The mind or experience or what?'

Certainly not the mind or experience. What's being said here doesn't come out of anything other than nothing. This is being talking to being; what you are talking to is what you are. There's no one here who's working this out – it just comes out. Tony Parsons sometimes thinks, 'What the hell? What's going on here?'

o   o   o

There's a fear that – say the penny drops – well I hope it will drop,

34

though I know I have no choice in the matter ... There's an anxiety that stuff would fall away and I might become an unbearable person to live with.

OK, so what?

And my partner might hate me.

But so what? Because if your partner needs the invitation in his life of you being unbearable, that will be your gift for him.

What is being talked about here is beyond the mind and heart of man. It's beyond understanding, it can't be understood. And it can't be related to goodness or badness. It's beyond all of that. But it also embraces all of that.

So what motivates you to come every month?

Nothing. There is no one who is motivated. The body/mind of Tony Parsons steps into the train and notices that it's getting off at the other end. It just happens; nothing is motivating it. There's no agenda going on here. All that's happening is nothing is speaking to nothing. There's no agenda or need in that, there's no motive in that at all. If there was, I would advise you all to leave right now, because it's just another manipulation. I'm not interested in you believing this. I mean, really, actually, you don't need to come back, because you are already the divine expression.

It's such an anticlimax!

Oh, it is. But that's one of the things that seekers are finding. Seekers want to find something amazing that will change their lives and make all their problems go away ... It is an anticlimax in one way – it's totally ordinary. Ask some people in this room who this has happened to and they'll tell you – it's absolutely ordinary and why doesn't everybody see it? But it's also magnificent.

Maybe I just haven't got the right personality.

It has nothing to do with you at all!

But there must be some people where the penny drops and others where it doesn't! You've already indicated that there are several people here where the penny has dropped – isn't there something in the character, the personality?

No, this has got nothing to do with the character at all. It has nothing to do with the person – it doesn't happen to the person. You see, it doesn't happen to Bill or Mary – it doesn't happen at all – it is what is. This whole existence is filled with only that, and all that gets in the way of that is the idea that Bill or Mary exists. When that drops away, there is what always is; that which is the one constant that never comes and never goes away. It is the constant unconditional love.

OK. But I have to realise that.

No, *you* don't – What you could come to see is that there's no one there to realise it; there just is seeing. In very practical terms, in terms of looking through the eyes, there's no one in this room seeing me – there is only seeing. The seeing that you think is going on from you is actually simply seeing. See from nothing – just let there be seeing. The strange thing is that that actually is all there is anyway. All that's over the top of it is some idea that you're there, that there is a person there.

Would the word 'impartiality' come into this seeing?

Well, yes, in a way, you could use the word 'impartiality'. It's impersonal, it's totally without judgement. It's flat seeing. At first it's a little bit disturbing because it doesn't feel like the thing we think it should be – all glossy and beautiful. It actually is impersonal, totally impersonal, and it's just out of nothing.

o   o   o

Can the separated self I call 'me' come to oneness through scripture?

Through the scriptures? Absolutely certainly not! In a way, you could say all the written words hold something of the secret, but it is really only ink on paper. It's just words again. The words here are totally inadequate; the words in my books and on those tapes are totally inadequate. And 'me' doesn't come to oneness – 'me' arises in oneness. There is only oneness and 'me' arises in that. So you will never be at one – there is oneness, with 'you' arising in that.

The mind finds it difficult to comprehend that.

The mind will never comprehend it because the mind is the tool of oneness to split everything into separation, into two. This is two – female and male; the whole creation is twoness – male and female. And awakening is the marriage of all of that in oneness. The mind is only an instrument and can never get anywhere near what we're talking about. It isn't meant to get near what we're talking about. That's why it's a good idea not to try to remember anything that's being said here, or even to listen. You don't need to listen – you *are* this.

On the one hand you're saying some really good things but you're also saying you've got no intention of being somebody who's spreading the word. And yet you're spreading the word.

Oh no, not at all! There's absolutely no intention here of being somebody who spreads the word! There are so many people around who have the intention of spreading the word it's untrue, and most of it is the confused word. The people who have the intention of spreading the word are spreading the mis-word – it's the teaching of the immaculate misconception. Because somewhere there's still a personal motive to speak to somebody and this is the ignorance.

And in a lot of cases there is a sincere belief that those people have attained something called enlightenment, and that they did it in a certain way; and there's a sincere wish to help other people attain something called enlightenment. The teaching is, 'You are a person who has a choice to do a, b and c' – usually a list – 'and if you follow a, b and c rigorously enough or seriously enough, you will attain what I have attained'. It has no relationship to awakening at all.

o   o   o

When there is a 'Yes!' to the words, is it source recognising source?

Yes, but it isn't something to do with understanding – it's more to do with intuition. It's like a jump, a leap, a sudden seeing of something that was already known. 'Oh yes – I know this!'

And is that more likely to happen by virtue of our coming here?

I think in some ways what goes on here (and elsewhere) is that the mind comes in, as I said at the beginning, with the intention of getting something – and then realises that it's not going to get anything, because actually there's nothing being given. It goes on coming, still with the idea of getting something, and it doesn't get anything … And it goes on and on until it just simply gives up. When there's a realisation that there's nothing to get, then what begins to be seen is this as it is.

This has nothing to do with detachment or non-identification this is to do with letting go of the seeker and discovering that what we are is living in this paradise. This is about a love affair. It's to do with a total intimacy just with the wonder of this. It's like a child on the beach building sandcastles, and there's nothing else that exists but the sand and the sea and the saltiness. That's all there is – there isn't anything else. It's the wonder of that simplicity, the wonder of this, which blows everything about concepts, about good and evil, out of the window. It's the timeless wonder of what we are.

So you've only really come here to remember something. And

yes, if you keep on coming, somehow what has been piled on top of that simplicity just falls away.

So it is about realising the nothingness?

Yes, you could use those words. It is the seeing of oneness. And in the end there's no one here seeing oneness – there's no one here seeing anything, in that way. There's no one here – there's just oneness.

So the letting go of somethingness?

It's the letting go of the sense that there's anything to find and it's the letting go of the one in there who's looking around looking for something. It's just simply letting there be seeing, letting there be hearing, letting there be smelling, letting there be touching, letting there be recognition of feelings ... Letting the feelings simply be seen without any sense that they need to change; they just are what is. Everything that arises is simply the beloved everything.

o   o   o

Say you walk out of this space and you see conflict in the road in front of you, two people are about to come to blows. Do you have a feeling, a sense, that you might involve yourself in that? Or would you step back?

Well, I'm English so I'd pretend nothing is happening! *(laughter)* There's no way of knowing – I couldn't tell you now if I'm going to raise this arm or not.

But do you get a sense of what I'm implying?

Yes I do. The mind is always endeavouring to find a formula a formula for good living, a formula for enlightenment. If you go on to the road and you see somebody beating up somebody else, would you stop them? That has absolutely nothing at all to do with what we're talking about here. It doesn't have any connection – good action, bad action – it's just in the world of the drama. Awakening has nothing to do with goodness.

The appearance of goodness can be very confusing. There was a lady who had two parrots who could speak, but the only thing they would say was, 'We are prostitutes and we'll give you a good time!' That's all they would say. She was quite worried about this and she went to a friend who said, 'I know a Catholic priest who happens to have two parrots himself. I would have thought that if you went to him and showed him your parrots, the two sets might be able to get together and yours could be influenced for the better'.

So she went to see this priest and he said, 'Well, I do have two parrots, Bill and Joe. They don't actually speak – all they do all day is count their rosaries. Each of them has a rosary and they pray in silence all day. I have never known such dedication. Why don't you put your parrots in with Bill and Joe and we'll see if they have a good influence on them?'

So she puts her parrots in the cage and they say, 'We're really hot prostitutes and we'll give you a good time!'

Bill says to Joe, 'You can throw the beads away now – all our prayers are answered!'

Brecon Residential
November 2002

A lot of smuggling goes on between Mexico and America. One day a Mexican rides up on a bike with a bag of sand on his back. The border policeman says, 'Stop! I want to see what's in your bag'. The man answers that there's sand in the bag. The policeman asks him to empty it, and sure enough, it's just sand, so he lets him through. This happens again and again, two or three times a week, and the policeman just knows that there's something funny going on.

One day the policeman's over the border in Mexico, having a drink in a bar, and this guy walks in. The policeman goes over to the Mexican and says, 'I've seen you at the border but I'm not a policeman now – let me buy you a drink'.

So they have a drink and he says to the guy, 'Now look, just to go back to what happens at the border. You ride up on your bike with this bag of sand and I have a look and always it's just sand. But I have this strong feeling that you're smuggling something. Come on, we're friends now – I'm not going to report you – just tell me what you're smuggling'.

And the Mexican says, 'Bicycles'.

What I like about the story is that it is very close to what we're talking about. In one way, the secret is hidden – and in another way it is totally obvious.

Because right now, that is all there is. Right now, here, that is what is happening. In these body/minds clear seeing is happening; there is just seeing. But somewhere in the mind there is an idea – and that is the whole drama – that there is someone sitting there seeing. That is the subtlety of this and the obviousness of it.

When awakening happens (as it does quite a lot now), one thing people say more than anything else is that what is now seen is totally obvious. It is *so* obvious. It is right next door to what you think is going on right now. You *think* that you are seeing me – in fact all that is really happening is that there is the seeing of me, or whatever it is that's arising. The difference between awakening and not awakening – between seeing and not seeing – is simply the seeing that there is no one there. There is no 'me'.

If you want to, you can close your eyes and try and find 'me'. What arises are sensations. There can be feelings inthe body, thoughts … It doesn't matter what it is that arises – a 'me' can't be found in there. Look for 'me' – it's not possible to find a fixed place, a fixed point that is 'me'. Where is your 'me'? Go on looking for 'me' and all that is actually found is sensations, bodily sensations, awareness of body, awareness of the thought 'I can't find me' …

And the strange thing is that that which is looking for 'me' is what you are. You are the one that is looking. What you are is oneness. Oneness is the seer, the seer of everything. Oneness is everything and sees everything as itself. All that has happened is that in some way or other we've been looking for something else, something personalised, an object called enlightenment; something that is out there and should come out of the sky and fill us up with a new energy; something that comes and adds to us.

In fact, what we look for is the loss of the energy of a 'me'. It is simply the loss of personal identity – which never ever was a reality anyway. We look for the loss of an unreality. Everything is lost, and in a way the 'me' is everything. We are rich people trying to find the kingdom of heaven. All the time there is a 'me' that has concepts about itself, the importance of life and the importance of finding enlightenment, we are rich people.

And all of that falls away, and there is nothing left but the seeing of this; just the clear seeing of sensations, of life apparently happening. That clear seeing comes out of nothing. It is as though there is nothing there, seeing life happening. Without any sense that what is happening needs to change, to be better or worse; without any judgement at all, or any sense that what is seen is going anywhere. And beyond clear seeing resides unicity.

So what you are looking for already is. What you are looking for is already this. Actually, all your life there has been clear seeing. What overlays that is the identification, as though there is a separate seer. And that overlay is also divine.

It is just a shift in perception from that to this. It is utterly simple, utterly direct and available. Enlightenment is totally available. Light is all there is. All these ideas that you have about climbing a mountain and meditating for twenty years, giving up desire … Awakening has nothing to do with any of that. Light is all there is. There is nothing that has to be done, simply because it is just the seeing of this. Who has to do anything about that? There is always this, there is only ever this. Wherever you go, there is only this.

Don't get the idea that awakening can only happen to people who've been intently seeking for years. There are quite a number of people, both here and in Holland, who've never ever been down any path or made any effort or been devoted in any way, and for whom awakening has happened and is apparently established.

The mystery of how the seeking drops away – both for people who are very devoted to it and also for people who aren't – is just unanswerable.

I don't know if anybody's read *Superconsciousness Revisited*? It's quite an interesting book by a psychologist which looks at the whole business of awakening – what he thinks happens and what happened to him, so he's not talking from ignorance. In one chapter there are quite a number of cases of people who have no more idea of what enlightenment is about than fly in the air; they just haven't been involved at all. And yet this new seeing has happened and has stayed with them.

So what I'm saying is that awakening has nothing to do with history. In a sense, a long-term seeker can collect many concepts and become what Christ called 'a rich man'.

Tony, without all the effort of seeking, it sounds like a lottery.

Yes, in a way you could say it does. It isn't, but that's how it sounds. But it's also possible to see that, actually, awakening doesn't happen to anyone.

That's all very well if it's happened to you!

Yes, but that is the reality of it. People appear to do the lottery and win it, but nobody does 'becoming awakened'.

But anyway, what to do, whether you think it's a lottery or not? If you think it's a lottery then you think it's a lottery. After it's happened, you see it isn't anything to do with it being a lottery, or something that happens to you.

Do you mean that all these years of effort have been wasted?

I'm afraid so! *(laughter)* Nothing is ever wasted, of course. You know that. Nothing is wasted, everything is just what it is. But whatever effort you put into this never brings anything other than the reinforcement of somebody putting effort into something which already is the case.

o   o   o

If you're in the clear vision and you're in the absolute consciousness, then as absolute consciousness you could awaken whom you want to.

Oh no, not at all. There's no way in which anybody can bring about another person's awakening because nobody is awakened, so you can't make somebody else awakened. All it is is the dropping away of the seeker, and nobody else can make anybody drop the seeker. You can tell them there's nothing to look for but they won't bloody well listen to you, I've noticed!

Surely it's your own play?

Whose play? Even after awakening there is no one there to choose or to make anything happen. And there's no need to make anything happen. Whatever seems to happen is only an appearance of the one.

But whose play is it?

It's nobody's play – it's just play. There is no one – there is no one out there! There really isn't – there's no one. There's just play.

But isn't it some form of intelligence?

There is intelligence but it's not an intelligence – it's just intelligent play.

OK, but this consciousness …

Hold on, you're talking about God, aren't you?

I'm not really talking about God – I'm just talking about the fact that it is something; it is being. It is something, or it's nothing …

It is both something and nothing. It's this. It isn't a consciousness from somewhere – this is, if you like, consciousness. This is life. There is simply life playing life, and there's nothing that's directing that and nothing that's choosing anything. There is no destiny. There's nothing going anywhere at all. This is simply life playing life.

And there is nothing out there that says, 'You will be enlightened', because there is no one who will ever be enlightened. You are enlightenment – you are that. This is that. And there's simply an idea that this isn't that. When that idea drops away, then what already is there is seen, by no one.

So there is no one who can therefore make awakening or clear seeing happen to another supposed person.

The whole idea of being able to enlighten somebody or transfer enlightenment comes straight out of the manipulative mind of the one who implies that that can happen through them; and for the one who wants it to happen. People go to teachers who will say that they can enlighten them, because that sounds like a very attractive idea. It never happens – it can't happen, because there's no one here to do anything to anyone else there.

You are totally alone; you always have been totally alone. And in a way, that's why it's the secret, because in a way it's apparently a totally personal secret, in that all the time there's a seeker, there's a secret on offer. That's the invitation. And for that seeker their invitation is totally unique.

Everything that's happening for you is a totally unique invitation for you to discover that there is only oneness. But no one else can move you any nearer to that through anything they do. They can't choose to take you anywhere nearer to what you already are. No one can, because it's a happening that's totally alone. The whole of creation is for you. That's absolutely true totally uniquely for you.

So you're alone but there's no loneliness.

No, there is no loneliness, except obviously before awakening. Afterwards, there is aloneness but you are living in love, so there's no loneliness because falling in love has finally happened; falling in love with everything. The perfect lover has been found because everything is the perfect lover. And this is all oneness.

Energetically really all that's happening is that in this room the nothing that is there, if you like, is seeing and meeting the nothing that is here. And energetically there is an expansion into that nothing. But all that you're really seeing is what you are. There's nothing that's coming from here to make any difference there. All there is here is the seeing of what you are. And in a way, because that energy is incredibly liberating, then that liberty is seen and expanded into. This is about expanding into love, really. But it isn't owned by anyone; none of this is owned by anyone. It's just seeing or not seeing.

You never actually move away from it – you live in the invitation, in that imminence. You *are* that imminence.

But there can be more openness to it within this setting.

Sure, because in a way coming here is like a prayer, like the one prayer. The only prayer there is is 'Make me nothing', if you like. 'Let me be nothing for seeing to happen'. So in coming here with that prayer, there is a certain imminence.

o o o

When you say invitation, Tony, that produces an idea of something that can be accepted or rejected, and that's not so because no one can do anything. Is that right? So it's not an invitation that can be accepted or rejected.

Well, it is in a way because actually the invitation is almost continually rejected. The mind doesn't see the invitation – the mind *can't* see the invitation because there's an image of a 'me' that lives in the mind, which lives in time. And you could say that the invitation isn't accepted because the invitation is timeless. We live in almost continual rejection of love. Another word for invitation could be grace.

But when there is acceptance … is there acceptance?

Again we're getting into a bit of a paradox, because all that really happens is that the supposed person or the imagined

47

separate being who picks up the invitation actually vanishes. The taking up of the invitation is the vanishing of the seeker.

But everything that arises is the invitation to see that what you are is the one. Most of the time we bypass that. We chase around the world doing our thing and looking for enlightenment and not noticing that the footsteps we take to the next retreat are actually the invitation, are actually the one, footstepping. The rejection or acceptance of the invitation cannot be chosen, it simply happens.

Invitation is one of those words that kind of sends me off on a tangent.

It's the nearest word I can get for that which can't be expressed. But in some way or other, all the time there's somebody looking for something, then everything is inviting them to see that they don't have to look for anything. If you can suggest another word, that's fine but I can't think of one, except grace … We live in constant grace.

Could you say it's the invitation not *to identify with whatever?*

Not really, no. It is the lover showing itself and it can be seen or not seen. It's not pushing you away – it's just inviting.

The prayer you talk about – who are you sending it to?

No one. The seeker is praying to itself, really; to what it is. The seeker is praying to its own nature – 'Please reveal yourself', let's say. 'I'm ready to give up everything for that'. Although people don't necessarily come here thinking that they're ready to give up everything, that's actually what is going to happen in the end. This is about giving up everything. Or you could say it's about giving up investment in an appearance. But it is a kind of death, and it seems like a threat because we're so used to living in this thing we think we know, the 'me'. So it feels like more than giving up an appearance …

o   o   o

The mind gets hold of the idea that what it's looking for is a state; what it's looking for is something that it can hang on to and fence in. Meditation is one of the ways in which the mind tries to establish such a state. The theory is – quite rightly, it seems – that if you sit and meditate, then it's possible that you can reach a state where there is no longer a meditator. So you could say you're reaching a state where there is no 'me'. And people can sit and formally meditate and find that there's a space where there is no meditator, where there's no one there any longer. That state can stay around for hours, minutes or seconds or whatever.

The difficulty is that thereafter the apparent meditator comes back and gets up and goes out into the kitchen to make a cup of tea, and there's a frustration because the state that was there is no longer necessarily there. There is also a meditation where one can create a state of bliss which can be very lovely, but when one goes off to do something or one comes back, then again that isn't necessarily there anymore.

The theory is that the more one can promote this state of there being no meditator or there being bliss, then maybe it will permanently stay there and you can live in bliss or live in there being no one. But actually, the whole thing is artificial in that it's based on the idea that enlightenment is something apart from what is normally known. 'There is a state called "no one" which is enlightenment. Therefore if I can capture that, I can somehow put a piece of fencing round it and maybe live in it'. The frustration from meditation is that it's like holding sand in your hand – it just runs right through. This kind of attempt to fix something is like trying to write on water.

What we're talking about here is something that actually already is the case. What we're talking about here is something that has never come and never goes away. It is presence, it is stillness ... The words don't express it, but it's not a state and it's not something that is here and then isn't here. It is actually all there is.

What's in the way of knowing that is you, is the mind, is the 'me', the 'me' that wants to find that state. And no amount of meditation, no amount of sacrifice or purification, nothing of that sort will ever allow that to emerge, because that doesn't need to emerge. And no amount of meditation or effort or purification will ever destroy the illusion of 'me', because the whole effort of trying to destroy the illusion of 'me' continues to reinforce 'me-ing'.

If you set aside the use of meditation as a method of purification and everything that is contained within that proposition, does it not, however, have some value, in that there is this nothingness, there is an appreciation, there is — you can't really call it an experience — but there is nevertheless an experience of the seeing of nothingness? Does it not provide some sort of confirmation?

Oh absolutely, though in a way that seeing of nothingness can happen in any situation. Certainly, if meditation is going to happen for that to be seen, then that's what will happen. What I'm saying is there's no way you can creep up on yourself; you can't creep up on awakening. There is no method that allows you to go on a journey towards what already is the case.

What often happens is that you do get that taste as it were, but the fact that you were doing a technique creates a subtle sense that there's something to be achieved. So it becomes such a tantalising barrier, because you know there's something there, but the sense of it not being what you already are is in fact reinforced by the fact that you're doing a technique in order to have it.

Absolutely. And the conditioning in our lives is such that that idea is very attractive. To become a good tennis player, you've got to practise every day and practise your backhand until it becomes a natural and strong stroke. And if you run five hours every day, you're going to become a good runner. It's like everything else we are conditioned to believe that effort will bring results.

Is that same danger not present here now as well? There's still a bunch of seekers here sitting in front of someone who doesn't have a system, or whose system is not to have a system.

Absolutely, but if we talk about it, if it's expressed, then there's a possibility the mind won't get entrapped so easily. Whereas in the atmosphere of meditation and meditation schools and those sort of systems, the whole thrust is towards somehow obtaining awakening. Let's be clear that what is suggested here is not to have or not have a system but to see that there is no one who can choose.

I was just thinking about what you're saying, and I thought awakening was about the mind coming to rest and just being.

The mind doesn't come to rest – the nature of the mind is not to be at rest.

But I thought you've said that the mind becomes acquiescent – which is exactly what I'd heard before in regard to meditation.

The mind finds its natural place and function. It doesn't come to rest but it takes its place in reality as a functioning tool, rather than trying to be the great guru.

When I first started meditating it was very difficult because there was all this mind-stuff, all this thinking, going on. And then there came a time when that wasn't there anymore and the mind was just very quiet. Now I don't know from what you're saying if that is just some induced state … I wouldn't say it was blissful particularly – it was just quiet and much easier to be, in that quietness.

There's nothing right or wrong with that – it's just that what you then have is a person who has a quieter mind.

So how would it be different with what you're describing?

51

The idea of somebody having a quieter mind bears no relationship to awakening. There's no relevance; there's just no connection between the two. It's like therapy. You can go into therapy and forgive your mother, so then you're a person who's apparently forgiven their mother. Or you can go and meditate for years and have a quiet mind – then you're a person who apparently has a quieter mind. Both of these are possessions. Awakening brings total poverty and absolute wealth.

Having a quieter mind makes life easier in the play and you get on better with people and don't have so many rows. You could say it makes for a more harmonious life ...

When you have someone who apparently lives a more harmonious life you have someone who apparently lives in a state of harmony. Of course, awakening can happen then too, but there is no one there who brought about that state or who can maintain it.

o   o   o

For someone who hasn't had the experience you've had, there's so much danger of trying to make it happen. For example, you can sort of bring the 'me' under observation and not work from it, but there's actually nothing we can do to change things. It seems hopeless.

It *is* hopeless. It's utterly and completely hopeless. It's even worse than hopeless – because hopeless in some way or other indicates that there might be somebody there who's hopeless.

o   o   o

It seems to me that you would like us all to be able to step free or however you'd describe it.

I wouldn't like you to – let's just go carefully here!

But I always have a feeling, with Michael and Roger, that you're so delighted for them, that that situation has arisen.

There is a delight that that's happened, but there's no one here who can make them or want them to be like that.

But there is a delight.

Yes.

So if it should happen for everyone here today who isn't there already, there would be a tremendous delight.

Yes, there would.

And that's all we can say.

Yes, except that I'd double the fee! *(laughter)*

o   o   o

In awakening, does the ego dissolve or is it still there and just transparent?

Everything's there.

Because I equate ego with need.

Yes, need is there as well, in the character, and also in the whole manifestation, the play of one, and I am that.

OK, that's something I was confused about, when you've said there is no one there to need other people. But need is still there, isn't it?

Yes, need is still there. You could say that there's just presence and in that everything arises, including need. But there's no longer a central figure in, let's say, Tony Parsons who needs something to fulfil what is already there, in the sense that there was before awakening. So there's nobody there centrally who needs anything, but need arises. The centre that was there before that wanted everything to come to it is no longer there. But Tony Parsons needs dinner or whatever – anything that arises.

This probably won't mean anything but it seems to me that it could be described as the clock has just stopped ticking.

Yes, it's the same thing – there is no longer any time factor involved, therefore there is no sense of a future or a past.

But the other thing about this is that it isn't really a personalised thing. Being in presence is being everything, so if it is being everything, then obviously need arises. And not just in this body/mind but in every other body/mind that happens to be present, that happens to be in that awareness. So I am everything in this room … There is only oneness, therefore what I am – which is oneness – is everything in this room. And there is need in this room.

I'm confused about this need. If you take the example of you needing dinner to satisfy a hunger drive within the body/mind, to me that would seem that there is still something central that is requiring something to be satisfied, something external to be taken in.

Yes, OK, well that's the point – there *is* nothing central. What arises is the need to satisfy a hunger drive – not to satisfy *my* hunger drive. We use language in such a way that we personalise need or suffering – 'I am suffering'. In clear seeing there is no one who is suffering and there's no one who's hungry – but hunger arises.

Tony, if everything that arises in every moment is just arising and falling away, and then the next moment there's another arising and falling away, in terms of the duality are there any links? Are there any laws that govern what's happening in the duality?

Well, of course in the end nothing's happening at all, but in the appearance of things arising, yes, they are governed by natural law.

What do you mean by that?

Well, the law of attraction, say – this is arising and is attracted to that. That law is the way in which manifestation works; it works within the laws of nature. If you cut a tomato with a knife, it cuts in half – there's a law in that. All the natural laws still apparently function.

And there are still reference points.

There is only being. There are no reference points in awakening, none at all.

But you'd have to have the reference point of your body/mind to satisfy that hunger drive … I'm struggling with this.

Well, if you want to call it a reference point, but all it actually is is the seeing of hunger arising and hunger being satisfied. If you think of the body as a reference point, that's up to you to think of it like that. But it's not seen like that here. All that's seen is a body; all that's seen is the apparent existence of a body which can feel hunger and eat and then not feel hunger.

I think what she means is if hunger arises, how do you know that the food has to go into this mouth and not into that mouth?

You *don't* know – it just happens. Functioning happens and it happens actually about a hundred times better than it did before. But there is no reference point – there are just things happening that are seen.

The difficulty with this is this idea of localisation, because one would think that if Tony Parsons' body is hungry and then Tony Parsons' body consumes something and isn't hungry, somehow that's something happening locally. But actually all it is is oneness, appearing as hunger and satisfaction. And it is very difficult at first, when all this begins to happen, because there's still such a conditioned idea of it being local. That's so powerful. We're so into this local feeling – we don't realise it isn't local at all – it is everything. Our body is the beloved, body-ing, and the chair over there is the beloved, chair-ing.

We're into this local feeling so much because we've carried this body/ mind with us since we were born, and I find it amazing that that could ever drop, with the body/mind still there. For that localisation to go must be such a shift.

Well it is, but you see you've used the word 'here' – the body is here. But actually the body isn't here – the body just is. When you say 'here', where is it near? It's near the person you think you are. When there is no one, there's just body, and it's not here.

OK, so what happens when that goes? I can't see how there could be no point of reference.

I know – there are no boundaries, there's no point of reference, there's just this.

There's no here then?

There's no here, yes. That's what I'm trying to say – there is no here, there's no there, there just is what is. Here, there and reference points are simply appearances, like gravity.

Talking like this can make it sound as though there's a continuous body, but there isn't – the body just appears and disappears all the time.

Yes, for instance right now you're aware of your body. At 3 o'clock during the night, there won't be any body. Even in the day, there are a lot of times when there is no body.

Like when?

Oh, come on! When somebody walks into the room or you're reading a book or are totally engrossed in a film … You're in something else, and there is no body.

o o o

56

Tony, if we take the analogy of the wave, when we were talking earlier on I had this feeling that maybe I'm just a constriction that arises and then disappears again. But how come when I arise again it doesn't rise in your form, say? How come that in the material sense it's always in this form? It seems odd that the wave always rises in this form.

Yes, it's miraculous.

Is that part of the mystery?

Yes, it's part of the mystery and part of the on-going drama and story about there being someone who is an individual separate from everything else.

The whole magic of there being nobody else like you in the world – when it's clearly seen – is a total celebration. But all the time it's seen as individuality, it creates a disquiet. It goes on confirming that actually there is someone there; there is a separate individual there. Because there isn't anybody else like you, then somewhere that reinforces the sense that you are separate. It's divine, of course – as I must go on emphasising this morning, obviously! It's divine because it's the lover presenting a situation which takes that seeker into love.

Every day, every morning, the wave forms and is saying, 'Look, this is what it's like in this separate world we've decided to play in! Isn't it a wonderful game?' And after awakening there's a celebration of the uniqueness of this creation, and there is no longer a need to find out anything about that. There are no questions about it anymore – it's just what it is.

But you can still celebrate the character?

Oh absolutely, for the first time, because the celebration is so free. It's a wonderful celebration first of Tony Parsons and thereafter, naturally, of everyone else. It's the two Commandments of Christ – 'Love God and love thy neighbour'. That's what he was talking about; he was talking about the open secret. 'See that you are all that is, and love that which arises in that'.

o   o   o

I remember at one time you were talking about the clarity versus a kind of encompassing. I can't remember it well enough to put it into words.

Well, I was at one time talking about the relationship between apparent men and women and masculine energy and feminine energy, where the masculine fears the fire and the feminine fears the impersonality.

That's right, yes.

What can happen in awakening is that people move into something which I'd call detachment or non-identification. It's not actually awakening but it is, you could say, an opening to awakening that happens; and in it, there is an awareness of objects arising. One lives in an awareness which is very detached from everything; it's non-identified with everything. But subtly there is still someone there who is aware of objects arising, so in a subtle way there's still a dualism.

This can happen more readily in the male energy than it can in the female energy, because the masculine likes to live in the ivory tower of cool and non-identified awareness. Often the masculine can stay in that, because it's safe and there is no intimacy there, like an ivory tower.

And what can happen in that situation is that life can come along and smash down that ivory tower, or that glass box, as I sometimes call it. Life breaks that box with passion or fire. The feminine represents earth and the fire and intimacy, and that's what breaks the ice-cold non-identification that the masculine can live in. But if that glass box can be broken, then what emerges is liberation – which is unconditional love, of course.

Liberation is not anything to do with non-identification or detachment – it is about a love affair. It's the ultimate love affair. It is the marriage of ice and fire. But let's be very clear that this arises in what is and it is not therefore necessary to be in a relationship. Relationship is only a representation of the awakening that is beyond it and yet embraces it. The apparent body/mind organism consists of both, the masculine and feminine polarities, as everything does.

On the other side, feminine energy, you could say, can have a very emotional sort of experience which is very powerful and has all the colour and fire of love, devotional love. But somewhere there isn't the impersonality there that the male energy has. And then what happens is that if there's a real marriage of clarity and passion, then again liberation can happen.

So really liberation is just a marriage. It isn't just a marriage it's *the* marriage. Fire and ice extinguish each other and the result is nothing awakening into everything.

What happens to someone who's caught in the fire, if the ice bit is like the ivory tower or the glass box?

They tend to stay in a highly emotional state (which isn't necessarily all over the place). There's a sense of great love but not great clarity. And they tend to communicate in that way.

The trouble with the halfway house situation is that to a certain extent there's still subtly someone there, and what can happen is that very often people get to the halfway house and think that enlightenment has happened and then start communicating it. They often communicate very sincerely, but the difficulty is that when there's someone still there, what can happen is that the one that's still there has an agenda, and that agenda is projected on to those who are being apparently taught and listening to that message. And whereas in full liberation the energy simply goes out and out and out, in the halfway house situation it can go out and then return back to the self. Of course, it is all the divine expression.

What's the eventual outcome of that?

Oh, it's what it is, it's just the divine game. If one wants to be dry or power-hungry or a big momma or a big poppa or whatever, then that's what happens. If people need to go to be with any of these appearances, that's the invitation they need. It's totally perfect.

But this doesn't mean to say that a man needs a woman or a woman needs a man, at all. You don't need to be married … Living alone, the male and the female energy is there anyway, in the one body/mind. That marriage can and does happen in one body/ mind, because in all of us there's the male and the female polarity. We all have the fire and the ice in each one of us. And it doesn't matter what your sexual orientation is – it has absolutely nothing to do with this.

o   o   o

I've just seen for the first time what the big question is that I'm carrying around, and it's 'What's it like to be enlightened?' I thought I had lots of questions but really it all boils down to that one.

It isn't like anything, because the whole question comes from 'What's it like for Tony Parsons to be enlightened?' and Tony Parsons *isn't* enlightened – nobody is. It's not a state; it's not something that is like something. In fact, the nearest you can get to it is to say it's like nothing. It's nothing.

o   o   o

Are the apparent gaps between the apparent thoughts that seem to occur in long periods of silence anything to do with anything?

No, they are the apparent gaps between the apparent thoughts. The thing is that the mind wants a formula – 'I've heard that if you can become aware of the gap in between thoughts, then that is a path to enlightenment'. There isn't anything much more nonsensical than that. People agonise over leaping into these gaps – 'Yesterday I was in six gaps! How about you?' 'Oh damn, I was only in four'.

It's putting the cart before the horse, isn't it?

You are absolutely right – it's putting the cart before the horse, because awakening is nothing, but when you're on the other side, you want to know what it's like. And there's no way you can ever know what it's like. And when it is there, there's no one to know what it's like.

You see, the answer to all questions really is 'There is only this, the seeing of this, just as it is'. So when one sits there and sees what is, or tries to see what is, that's fine. But subtly the mind can come in and say, 'Oh, it's all very well that there's just seeing what is, but isn't there any more than that?' The mind always wants more. But if you can just stop the world and see what is, and then *also* see that the mind comes in and says, 'It's got to be more than this', then you see the basic drama, let's say, that's going on all the time; the play of just seeing this and then the mind saying, 'This isn't enough – I want more. This isn't enlightenment – I want more'.

And then, as the agitation of the mind is seen, that agitation begins to dissipate in that seeing. Just seeing the mind coming in and saying, 'There's more – there's got to be more than just sitting on a seat'. That's when that agitation begins to dissipate, because simply seeing the mind's activity gradually slows it down.

Then there's just the seeing of this, and there's a taste of sweetness about just seeing this. There's a sweetness about it because time has actually stopped – there is no time, there's just seeing this, the sitting in this. This sounds like a process, but it is only ever apparent time meeting the timeless.

○   ○   ○

At the moment, listening to what you're saying, it feels like there's a constant sense of insecurity, which really gets on my nerves, because on the one hand it feels comfortable – on the other hand it feels more uncomfortable than ever.

Absolutely, because you're sitting on the edge of timelessness. To let go of the mind and discard the mind, or just see the mind trying to agitate and just sit in this, this is threatening.

It takes a lot of confidence away, because it seems like I'm losing some of the things that I was leaning on before.

Yes, you're losing everything here. We have a confidence about what the mind tells us and we listen to it and are guided by it because we think it's highly intelligent. The mind is often a highly intelligent conman, actually. We listen to it and it does comfort us and reassure us. What you're now doing is dropping that.

It feels like there's not much I can do about it.

No, but there again, just see also that fear, the fear of being threatened. Just see that – that's another thing that's arising. So there's this – there's the mind saying, 'Oh, this is not very important' – and there's the seeing of the mind saying, 'Oh, this isn't anything – what's this?' And then there's fear – the mind frightened by the idea of the discarding of the mind. For once we see the mind as it really is, a story in time, trying to drag us back into the world of time where it can run the show.

I really have a sense of this not enoughness – it's a really strong sense of it.

The mind wants enlightenment or what we've come to believe in as a picture of enlightenment, and the seeker fears that what he's

62

going to find is going to be totally ordinary. And it is – it's no big deal. It's not what the mind would like to discover … But subtly the seeker knows that what he's looking for is totally ordinary and immediate and natural.

It's like one of those Zen stories where someone's looking for a lion and finds a mouse.

Yes, absolutely. However, it will be discovered that it's the wonderful mouse!

Totnes
September 2002

A conversation about teachings

The subject of teachers is something that's been confusing the hell out of me for quite a while. There are all these different characters around who are in a sense in the same position as you are – they're sat in the chair out front, we're sat here; they're writing the books, we're reading them.

I've been fascinated by this possibility they call enlightenment for years and years and years. I've done a certain amount of research into it – reading the books, listening to the tapes, going to see various people and so on. I was down in 'The Spiritual Bookshop' every day reading the books, because I can't afford to buy them. (They don't mind – they've got a comfy chair in there!) And I'd just sit there every day reading all these books, trying to puzzle out what the hell's going on here with this enlightenment thing.

It means a fair bit to me, and I've had all sorts of confusing paradoxical experiences with this thing myself. I was with Andrew Cohen for a few years, so I've had previous experience of being with one of these teachers ... And I'm more confused than ever.

Yes, that doesn't surprise me!

I'll tell you, the confusion I'm on about is this. Having tried to look into it, I don't feel that many of these teachers are just impostors, that nothing happened to them, and that they're sitting there pulling the wool over your eyes.

No, no.

I also don't feel that they're convinced that something's happened to them but actually it hasn't – which is another possibility. I think something has happened to them. That's why they're sitting in the chair and that's why they're tumbling out the books and that's why people are coming flocking to them in large numbers. Something has happened to them.

In one sense, I can see that there's a kind of connection between what's happened to all of these different teachers; and in another sense, they all seem to disagree – including yourself – with each other on various things. But there does seem to be a common link in what's happened to these people. There seems to have been a life-shattering episode that happened at some point in time – which seems to me to have been that their previous sense of identity has shattered.

Ah, yes … All right, let's go on. There's a little hook there but that's all right. Go on.

In other words, I'm saying I don't think they're all fakes; I don't think they are phonies. There probably are a few around – I'm not really sure but something seems to have shattered these people's sense of who and what they are. And it seems to me that, following this shattering episode, they are completely different to how they were before. And they often start teaching at that point.

Often the thing that seems to me to pull the crowds is not what they're saying or writing, but rather that just sitting around and being with them can have all sorts of strange effects on people. And I've experienced that first-hand a few times, and I think that's what's got me into it in the first place, probably.

So basically, I suppose, where I've got to is, are there different kinds of enlightenment around? It's almost got to the point now for me where it seems that every single person who's ever got enlightened is a completely different model of the thing. Which is not what I'd originally assumed they would be exactly the same, I would have thought originally. But I've now got to the point where it seems that every single one of them is a completely different kind of model.

And has a different message, do you think?

Well, as I said, I still think that there are certain central threads that run through these teachings, but there are many things that the teachers seem to disagree about. For example, your views on meditation as I've read them in your book totally conflict with other people's. Other teachers might say, 'You should meditate three or four hours a day'.

And so we can go on – you don't have to go through the list.

No, that's just an example. I wonder if you can throw some light on all of this.

Of course, for many people, they have some kind of personal spiritual experience, and this convinces them that they have become something called 'an enlightened person'. There is no such thing, but still they often communicate a teaching of personal attainment and claim that they can help others to reach a similar state.

Let's keep it at meditation for the moment and let's say quite a lot of those people have meditated or been involved in a process of some kind. What then happens is that they seem to move out of the sense of there being a 'me' and they go into a state of deep detachment. That is the initial pre-opening to enlightenment for many people. This isn't fixed, but let's be very simple about it and say that for most people non-identification can happen.

It's a shattering experience, as you quite rightly say, and it's *almost* totally liberating – almost. What is seen is that the world appears as objects arising and then falling away; and then other objects arising and falling away. That is a deep detachment, and it is an opening to enlightenment. The difficulty is that people don't know that there's a final letting go, and so they rush out and give satsangs. What they do is they go out and basically they say, 'I did this in order to attain enlightenment. And if I did this, you could do the same thing'.

There are many methods taught for achieving enlightenment.

There's clearing chakras, being celibate, being pure, being incredibly honest, dying for enlightenment, not caring about enlightenment ... There are almost as many different ways as there are people who think they have attained that point of enlightenment. However, what has happened hasn't become embodied.

OK, so what's the next step?

Nisargadatta put it in beautiful words. What he said is absolutely key to your question. He said, 'Knowing that I am nothing is wisdom ...' So they've reached the point of wisdom. And I'm not decrying that – this is big stuff. I tell you, when it happens to you – big time! It's amazing! But there's another step which goes beyond wisdom – which is absolute love. And Nisargadatta said, 'Knowing I am everything is love' – that's the other part of the statement. And that is the total disintegration of any sense of a permanent or fixed 'me'.

Whilst there's detachment, there's still a subtle sense of something that is aware of everything. You watch things arise and there's a sense of there being something that is detached that sees things arise. So when you go out to teach, what you do is you talk to someone about something that they can attain, which will give them the wonderful liberation of watching the world arise. And it is wonderful. It's a deep detachment, a non-identification. It's wonderful and it seems totally free – but, subtly, there's still someone there. It is what I call the glass box of detachment.

The other face of enlightenment is devotion, so you get teachers who have developed a strong emotional heart energy without the balance of the impersonal. These 'teachers' can often affect people's emotional centres.

And nearly all teachings talk to someone about something that can be attained.

When love appears and it shatters that glass box and there is simply love, then there is no way that there is any communication to anyone or that there's any way you can teach anybody anything. Because what is seen is that they are absolutely divine as they are. This is unconditional love.

So how can anyone tell you to meditate or sing mantras or be serious or be honest or any of those things? How can anyone tell you that, when already you *are* that? All that's going on here is that I'm telling you it's already like that; you already are oneness; you are already that.

That's the difference. And there are a handful of people in the world who are talking like that, who are that.

The reason why I'm so interested in these enlightened characters and have been for quite some time is because of this wanting to get enlightened myself.

Yes, absolutely.

I tried Buddhism and I wasn't sure about that. Then I tried Andrew Cohen, and that went horribly wrong. And then it was, 'Bloody hell, what am I going to try next?' So for several years I've really been just trying to enquire into what the hell this thing is. And the main way that I've done that is by enquiring into what enlightened people are like. So for quite some time now, I've been more interested in the accounts of what's happened to these people, trying to see what they're like.

This kind of enquiry – what the hell is going on with these enlightened characters? – reached a certain peak and sort of accelerated a few months ago, which is why I was sat in 'The Spiritual Bookshop' every day reading books, even some of them that bored me. It was like, 'What's going on? What happened? Where? With whom? I want to know, I want to understand this thing'.

Funnily enough, one of the books that I pulled off the shelf was yours, The Open Secret, *and that has opened up to me a whole new thing other than this intellectual enquiry as to what's going on. Something else is going on here between me and you, as far as I'm concerned.*

But something I'd like to bring up from what we've been talking about – and I mean this genuinely and in a very sort of solid way – is the question of whether or not I still want to be enlightened ... I'm not sure anymore.

That's exciting!

Yes, it is! And I've started to realise things about myself and the way that I've been looking at enlightenment, the way I've been looking at these enlightened teachers as role models and almost parental role models. And it's interesting, some of the things that were being said here right at the beginning of the day about 'You're already perfect' and 'It already is as it is' and so on, because that totally conflicts with this seeker who wants to get enlightened, who wants to be something other than he already is. And my poor old mind's going, 'I can see both sides, I can see both arguments!'

But another thing which is really interesting to me is that when I was reading The Open Secret, *I think one of the reasons why it really resonated with me from word 1, page 1 ... It was like, 'Bloody hell, I'm going to buy this one!'*

Hooray! Another seven pounds! *(laughter)*

If anything, what it was resonating with was my own experience, because I have had experiences and a sense that something in me already knows this. I had this strange sense as I started reading your book, almost as if I'd written it.

I've heard that before – 'I'm reading my own words'.

Yes. It was a kind of sense of self-recognition. And what it certainly did in a less mysterious way was remind me of my own highest experiences or deepest experiences. That's why, with most of it, I didn't need to go through any intellectual thing about whether or not it's true. It was just self-apparently true; I knew that.

The one side of it that I feel is not my own experience and has not been my own experience is when you speak about this overwhelming love.

When you speak or write or somebody talks about 'There is not really a "me" ' and all that kind of stuff, I actually have some sense of that; I know what you're on about there. You just said that the difference between one type of teacher and another is something to do with love ...

Yes, it is.

And in a sense I feel that that's what hasn't happened to me. And there's almost a dryness sometimes in my own wisdom, if you like. Reading through The Open Secret, *I think it was this love side of it that really kind of broke my heart and appealed to me.*

And back to whether or not I want to get enlightened, and whether or not I'm perfect as I am, the reason why people want to get enlightened is because they're suffering.

Yes.

I've been through awful anguish – I know what despair's like and I know how serious depression can get and all that kind of thing. If there's one thing that I've felt has been missing from my inner life – which is why I got into this – it's love; it's a loveless condition. And I think when you hear enlightened teachers talking about love and this unconditional love, that's the kind of thing that really ...

So again, I'm back to saying that you have something that I don't have.

No. Let's just stop there for a moment, because it's the other way round – *you* have something that I don't have. What you have is seeking – you still have an apparent someone who is looking for something. Awakening is simply the dropping of seeking. What drops away is the one that's looking for something. Awakening is absolutely purely and simply the discovery that there's nothing to look for. And therefore, out of that (and there's nothing you can do about that until it happens) – out of that not looking and realising that this is it, comes love. There isn't anywhere to go, you know. This is it, and you are it. I am looking at love; I am looking at the divine expression. That's falling in love ... That's what happens.

But at the moment, there's still somebody in there who's looking for that. So the love has not yet become apparent. When you mentioned the dryness, the kind of arid desert, that's where a lot of people are stuck, because there's something still dry even about being in that world of detachment. The lover isn't there; the love isn't. The love hasn't totally blown away that subtle sense of me looking for something.

Wherever you go and however many of these books you read down there ...

I've stopped, by the way!

But most of these books speak to a presumed someone who needs to attain or find something. Awakening, however, is only about the dropping of the one that's looking for something.

And how does that come about?

I can't say – there's no one who can say. As a little child, you weren't looking for anything. As a little child, you were in total love. Everything was just what it was. And then the game of separation began. And from that very moment of separation, you were looking – 'Oh, I've lost it! Where's it gone?' You were looking for love; you were looking for what you are. And now you've come to discover that you don't need to look anymore because everything you're looking at is that. It's absolutely as simple as that, and there's no one there who can do anything about that.

That's the other thing – there is no one. When you go to someone else who says to you, 'Look, you can choose to do this or that to find love', just forget it; it's just nonsense. These people are sincere, no question – but there is still a misunderstanding because there's still a subtle 'me'. So they're always talking to a 'me' and they're teaching about becoming. The open secret is speaking to 'I am'.

It's interesting, this thing about seeking versus non-seeking. I've had several really fascinating conversations over the past few months with old friends who are into all of this, and this subject has come up in every single conversation. Basically, I've always ended up coming down on the side of seeking and them of non-seeking. And this is despite the fact that I've read your book and all that kind of thing. I'm still sticking with what I feel …

Can I just interrupt there? What I'm talking about is beyond both. What I'm talking about is the realisation that there's nothing you can do about seeking or not seeking. What I'm saying to you is that there is no one there. And if seeking goes on and meditating goes on and clearing the chakras goes on and being honest goes on, that is what's going to happen.

There is no way to discover this … Also, it isn't that there is no way – there is no one that can discover this; there is no one that can be a certain way or be another way. So just forget about seeking and non-seeking.

I'm still saying to you that awakening is the dropping of the one who thinks there's something to find. I'm not therefore saying, 'Stop looking for it'. I *can't* say to you 'Stop looking for this' – there isn't anyone in there I can talk to who can choose.

The seeking can be seen as just something else arising?

Yes, the seeking is something else that's arising. There is no one in there it's arising for, but if I start to tell you to seek, I'm actually reinforcing the idea that there's someone in there who can make a choice. And if I tell you to stop seeking, I'm also reinforcing the idea that there's someone in there!

You've said about The Open Secret *that there are a couple of things in there that perhaps you'd change because they might be misleading. I wonder if you could say more about that?*

Well, I think any book, any words are misleading, really. Any words mislead, because words tend to express subject and object. If you read that book, it somehow still gives the impression that presence or whatever it is that we all long for is something attainable; it's like an object that is attainable. And to a certain extent it comes across as if there's some sense that I was choosing for things to happen – in describing the walk across the park, for example, when I 'chose' to watch my feet. Whereas really I only apparently chose to watch my feet.

When I read that book now, I think a lot of it is fine but some of it still is not really clear. No written word is clear – it is simply an attempt to point to something that is beyond it.

Going back to the seeking versus non-seeking, I think the reason why it keeps coming up in conversation is because there are a lot of books around where that issue is being put forward. I've talked to several people who are quite into all of this in one way or another, and they tell me that they've stopped seeking, and they feel I'm a bit of an idiot because I still am seeking. And although certainly – when you *talk about not seeking or if I read in your book about not seeking – I get a beautiful sense of what you mean, what I've found with most of the people I've been talking to is they've just stopped seeking.*

It's another agenda.

They haven't found anything. Usually because some kind of spiritual authority figure or other has convinced them into it, they've stopped the seeking. It's just left them empty-handed, as far as I'm concerned. And actually I don't really believe them.

Maybe they've stopped seeking in order that they can find something!

Yes, there's something not quite right. So I've found myself, strangely enough, paradoxically, sticking up for the other side in these conversations and saying, 'Look, if you want to stop seeking, that's fine. But you haven't

73

found what you were looking for'.

Really, in another way, there's no such thing as a non-seeker. Everybody in the world is seeking, and what they're seeking in the end is oneness. What they're seeking is the lover, what they're seeking is what they know they long for. But they look for it in different ways, like lots of money and lots of girlfriends, lots of this and that … Everybody is a seeker and what they seek is absence.

All the time there is a 'me' then there is a feeling of disquiet.

Tony, I assume that when you were 21 and walked through the park, was it fully embodied then?

No, no. It took years for embodiment to take place! But this can all happen in one go. There are people for whom the whole thing is over in one seeing, especially at this apparent time.

We were talking about teachers earlier and you were saying that there's an awakening that's happened to some of these teachers which is incredibly liberating and, more to the point, they start having an incredible effect on people around, which is why they start teaching. And from the point of view of the seeker who comes along (like myself to Andrew Cohen all those years ago), to bump into somebody like that – the kind of discrimination that you'd have to have, not to get sucked into that kind of … Looking back on it, it would have been impossible.

It was totally divine. It was absolutely what needed to happen – even if it means that confusion comes out of that. If the confusion needs to come out, it comes out, and then clarity follows that. It's all divine, it's all the one.

And of course, the thing that's most attractive to the mind is the idea of doing something. So if you get those sorts of people who are in that halfway house, with that sort of energy, teaching you to do something, it's a far more attractive message than this – this is *not* an attractive message. That's why people like Eckhart Tolle have such a huge audience. His original message actually is very simple, but it's still a teaching about something that you can apparently do.

I think one of the things that seems to be inherent in all of this as well is that in the relationship between someone like myself and someone like Andrew Cohen (I'm just using myself and him as examples), there's a whole thing there about superiority and inferiority. I have been coming to realise recently – probably to do with meeting you – some of my own reasons and motives for getting into this in the first place. And I don't like some of it, because I think it is wrapped into this whole thing of wanting to be superior to how you are and how other people are. You get into this whole thing of who's more enlightened than who.

That's so powerful. 'Somehow I am special and I should really go to the most special guru of all, the most important one, because that's how I want to be'. Of course, the other game is that your master is so special that you can never be like him or her – and therefore you can remain a disciple and thus avoid awakening.

And even within one teacher's structure, there are some students more special than others; there are inferiority complexes, there are superiority complexes … It's a mess. But I think I've started to realise recently that some of the drive behind my own search, which has been going on since I was very young, has been for sure this desire to be a superior being.

Oh yes, there's no question about it – the attraction of joining the Enlightenment Club.

And to be a teacher or a guru. In many people's minds – including my own perhaps, up until recently – being enlightened and being a guru are synonymous. I think that perhaps actually it's being the guru that some people want more than anything – the adulation …

So the big thing for me was the idea of getting something from someone who already had something. But meeting you, I've never ever had a sense of that. You've never suggested to anyone that that's the case.

The whole thing about awakening is not getting something.

We grow up wanting to get things; the mind always wants to get things. It's a bottomless pit. When we hear about enlightenment, we think it's something we can get. And enlightenment or awakening is not getting anything – it's actually losing everything.

It's very confusing, the subtlety of some of this, because some of these teachers that we've been talking about will speak with great clarity about the subjects that we've been talking about, along the same lines that you've been talking about them.

Yes, I know.

And for an ordinary individual not to get lost in that ... You might as well call it impossible; I think it virtually is.

You don't need to.

Also, you'll find that the things that you're saying – the others have said the same things. So it's not as simple as 'Now I know because Tony Parsons will tell me what Andrew Cohen never told me'.

Oh yes, absolutely. There are quite a lot of them that talk in a non-dualistic way at times.

Andrew Cohen will tell you, for example, that you don't get enlightenment. He'll tell you, for example, that you lose everything – you don't gain anything; it's not you – there isn't a 'you' and all that kind of thing. It's all in his teaching as well.

Yes, and it is quite common to hear so-called 'teachers' using non-dualistic language and then directly contradicting the real meaning of non-dualism by recommending processes and practices to presumed individuals. Many highly revered gurus and teachers, past and present, are classified as communicators of the advaita-vedanta tradition by the so-called experts and the general public, when in reality their teaching is dualistic. This kind of contradiction is either rooted in a deep ignorance about the nature of liberation or it comes out of a need to satisfy a personal agenda.

Can I clarify something that I think you've said? It appears that some people who come and see you have become the same as you.

Well, there is only oneness, but in simple language, yes, they've awakened.

So it's working?

You could say that.

So they've found what they were looking for. To be quite honest with you, if what you're saying is true – and I don't disbelieve you – it's unique, as far as I'm aware.

I don't think it necessarily is – I think that it does happen elsewhere.

I don't know of anywhere else.

Oh yes, it does. It's happening more and more now.

One thing that I've noticed about some of these teachers, gurus, whatever you want to call them, including some of the ones that I admire ... I think there have been some awful cock-ups made along the way in sending other people out to teach. Mistakes have been made.

Mind you, that's all divine.

Yes, but we've got to talk about this! So I came to the point, over the years, with my own run-in with Andrew Cohen as a guru, that I gave up on gurus. Apart from the fact that I had a terribly traumatic experience with one of them and then read loads of books about other people's traumatic experiences with others, I came to the conclusion that it doesn't work.

Well no, it doesn't. It's not working here either.

What do you mean?

Well, there isn't anything that can work. All that happens here is the possibility that you can lose everything.

London
September 2001

So, in this apparent world we live in – only apparent – in this appearance of a world that we live in, this is an amazing time to be around, because there is a sea-change happening. And it is partly to do with the demolition, the breaking down, of the idea that a guru or a spiritual teacher is somehow special.

There are still so-called gurus or spiritual teachers who want this idea to go on being maintained. There are still even quite young people teaching who take up this position of being special; and they create ashrams and they somehow become exclusive and untouchable. You can't ring them up and just have a chat with them about the weather. They are somehow 'over there'. And the sense is – when you're with them – that you can't get near to them.

This has been going on for thousands of years, really, and even until recently there has been this sense of them being 'over there' and me being 'over here'; me watching them and sitting and thinking how amazing they are, and how I will never – ever – be like that.

This is our own creation. This is how oneness has played it, until recently. The game has been for people to believe that they can never be like the figure they see who they think is awakened.

But there is a sea-change; things are changing. There are actually people communicating about awakening who are ordinary, who are not trying to sell anything, who are just friends. Friendship is happening in this whole thing, and that's because, somewhere, the people who are coming to hear about this wonderful news are beginning to see that it's their own message; it's theirs. They're beginning to see that they don't need a guru, they don't need a spiritual teacher. There's an opening in people's awareness, in people's understanding, where they are beginning to see … and are ready to see … and are ready to open to the possibility that they don't need anyone or anything.

Because they don't. Nobody needs ever to come here again *really*. You don't need to come to anybody to hear that you are the divine expression just as you are. Simply as you are – that is the divine expression. It doesn't need to change, it doesn't need to be better or worse or different – it is exactly as you are. That is the light manifesting. That is oneness being you, living through you.

So forget about the neurosis that you think you have, forget about the feelings of inadequacy that you have. I'm no more adequate than you are. I'm no different than you. The only difference is that there is a seeing that there's nothing to ask. There's a seeing that there is no separate 'me' here, and that there's nowhere to go. There's a seeing that this is it.

And more and more people are beginning to open to that, to see that. More and more people are coming to hear that just as they are is the divine expression.

And it's not special or exclusive, this awakening … it is the natural way.

Tony Parsons has to pay the bills and Tony Parsons can get angry. Tony Parsons can do anything and feel anything that anyone else in this room can feel. Anger arises. Boredom arises. Greed arises. It's fine! That's the game. That's the film that's going on, that's the drama that's going on. It is simply seen that what happens isn't happening to anyone.

But, for this *(pointing at self)*, there's no more looking for anything else. There is a total acceptance and falling in love with simply this as it is, knowing that there's nowhere else to go. There is no need to go anywhere else, and there's nothing to chase. Life is simply being life.

Nothing has to become anything else. No one in this room has to become any other way, has to become 'more perfect'. Nobody has to still their mind, nobody has to drop desire, nobody has to kill their ego. What's wrong with ego? It's part of the drama. It is the absolute, ego-ing. How can oneness become more or better?

All it is is a seeing. It's a seeing that's beyond you looking at me. All it is is sensing that which watches you looking at me ... in this. In this there is that which knows what is happening.

So it isn't anywhere else. At the end of the afternoon, after three hours, you are not going to be anywhere nearer it, because there is always only this. And when you go home tonight and meditate for three hours, you're not going to be any nearer either, because there will still be the watcher watching you trying to meditate to find the one that's watching you trying to meditate to find the ... *Really*. Everyone in the whole world is in meditation. No one is nearer or farther away from their original nature.

And the sea-change is this dropping of the idea, this dropping of the projection, this dropping of, in a way, the escape of going to see very special people who wear wonderful robes and speak very softly and kindly and listen to vegetarian music and drive up in big cars and have entourages. To go and see them is a means of avoiding what you are, because the mind will say, 'I can never be like that, so I will go on coming and talking about this and listening to this wonderful person so that I'll never have to drop this little "me" that goes around watching these wonderful people. I'll never have to drop that little "me" and discover my original nature'. They become permanent disciples.

In a way, when we go to see these special people, we're still avoiding, we're still seekers. These special people turn us more and more into seekers; their whole energy is to produce more and more seekers.

I'm saying to you, there is nothing to find and you won't find it through this *(pointing at himself)* – it is already there, there's nothing to find.

This is a difficult message to accept. For some people it's quite difficult to give up seeking because actually it's a very nice thing to do. In a way, it's the most valid, the most worthy occupation there is.

But I'm saying to you, if you really want to find, find it in this. No amount of meditation, no amount of stilling the mind, no amount of discipline can ever bring you one cubit nearer to what you are, because it simply reinforces the idea of seeking. It simply reinforces the idea that there is a 'me' that can find something over there. And anyway, there is nowhere to go.

Give up. Simply give up and rest in that which is already the case. It is the seeing of this; it always has been this, as it is. It's very simple, it's very ordinary – and it's magnificent.

The other thing that's happening now, it seems, is that the 'event' is not important. Thirty, forty, fifty years ago, when awakening happened, it was an event. And before that, for thousands of years, it was an event that was announced, and it hit the participant with a huge explosion – a huge explosion of awakening. But what is happening now is that people are becoming so aware and understanding of the nature of this that that explosion doesn't have to happen anymore. There's not that sudden change from one thing to another.

People are already open to this. And some people are simply realising that awakening has already taken over, and there's a freedom there. In sleep, too, when we sleep at night … Once there's an opening to this discovery, then in sleep, in deep sleep when there is no one, then this takes over and that body/mind wakes up to see that already there is just the light, just the awakening, just the realisation.

So don't look for the event; forget about 'It's going to happen tomorrow afternoon as a major event that I will remember'. Just forget that; you don't need that anymore. It may be that for some people that would happen, but for most people now there is just a moving into that seeing, clear seeing that all there is is this.

Who is it then who wakes up?

No one wakes up. Awakening is not actually anything that happens to anybody; clear seeing becomes apparent when there is nobody. Awakening is the dropping of the sense that there is anyone. The illusion of the separate entity drops, then there is what is already the case – light. It is then seen – by no one – that there is no one and nothing that needs to become liberated.

And that is the same as seeing? Just seeing? The one who thinks he's seeing falls away and there is just seeing?

There is just being.

o   o   o

It's often been said that there is a seer behind everything, or that's how people have viewed it. That still gives the idea that there is something there. But occasionally, with a bit more clarity, it's been described as 'There is only seeing'. There isn't a seer but just seeing.

That's it. Or being – there is only seeing or being. That's all there is.

Without a seer.

Yes. There is only light, there is only no thing. You could say there's only spaghetti, really ... These words, those books, that tape ... Something else is going on in this room but the words are so far away from it. What can happen here is that people come with ideas about what they are and what enlightenment is, and it's possible that that can be blown away by the clarity. But that's only understanding and understanding is nothing. Awakening is totally beyond understanding.

This is about children. What we're talking about here is the wonder of this. We've put it on a shelf somewhere and taken down another thing from the shelf called adulthood. That's all right, that's absolutely how it should be. But at some point or another a lot of people have the courage to take that other thing off the shelf again – the childhood, the wonder – and give up this idea of adulthood.

What is wonderment, as the opposite of adulthood?

In these terms, adulthood is the idea of somebody quite important who's fascinated by the idea that they have a life which they can change by their own choice and make better or worse. The idea of separate individuality is what for me adulthood is about. Childhood is about childlikeness, which is the wonder of this.

This is wonderful – you're sitting on a miracle, you drink and breathe in wonder. That's all that's happening. That's all that's always happening. It's always happening – the beloved has never left you because you are the beloved. And everything about you is the beloved. The only difficulty is that you don't think it is.

One thing I was reminded of when I was reading As It Is – *there's a bit where someone's asking you something and you throw down a jumper and you say, 'This is it'. It reminded me of the story of when the Buddha was sitting with various monks and he held up a flower. And one of them got it and just responded with a smile. It seems to be the same thing – it seems to all come back to that.*

83

Absolutely. And a flower is one thing, but dogshit is also the same thing. In fact, you see the point is that everything is from the source, everything's from what you are, everything's from unconditional love. So this wall is the beloved, wall-ing. It appears to be a wall, which is in a story called building houses for people to live in; that's the appearance. It's simply the lover, the beloved, in the form of a wall.

All the time you're sitting on and looking at and drinking and smoking and driving in the invitation.

Do you watch television?

Yes, absolutely. But there's nobody watching television television is watched. The idea that there's some way to behave is just nonsense. The idea that there's some way one should behave in order to reach something ... there's nothing to reach. The idea, the teachings that say one should be honest, completely honest with everyone; one should be serious about enlightenment ... It's so ridiculous because there is no such thing.

o   o   o

Can I ask, is there a magic key to waking up?

No there isn't – only seeing that this is it. The magic key in a way is the dropping of the idea that there's anyone there who can find a magic key and that there's any magic key to find. You are that.

It's going back to just giving up the identity.

If it's possible, yes. But you can't give up your identity.

Getting everything out of the way ...

You can't do that. You can't drop your identity.

That's what I'm finding!

The intender can't intend not to intend. What we're talking about here is coming to the realisation of helplessness. Not that *you* are helpless, because there isn't anyone there. Isn't that wonderful?

You can't do anything, you've never done anything. There is simply this. Come to see that whatever is happening, right now, is just happening and there's no one there it's happening to. Just let that be there. Just drop that guy or that woman who's been running around and sitting on your shoulder and telling you how you should do things. Just drop it and sit there and feel like nothing. Just feel like nothing. There's nothing. *(Someone coughs)* All there is is a cough.

It's so immediate, it is nearer to all of you than you are. You're sitting there looking at this – let there just be seeing. No one is looking – let there just be seeing.

I know you said there's no person, but is there anything that says that it's time for a particular person to wake up?

No, there is no time and there's no one to wake up. You are already that. It's just that you think you're in a lifetime that's going to last 75 years, and you think, 'Will I wake up on November 4th?'

Yes, 'How much longer is it going to take me?' (laughter)

No, it doesn't happen, it isn't happening, it never will happen – it already is that.

Is the idea behind karma and reincarnation just an invention then?

Yes, that's part of the appearance. It has no meaning at all.

It actually then doesn't exist. It's not as though it exists at another level or it's outside of our area of awareness – it's just not there?

It is all simply appearance. It's just another way of reinforcing the illusion of there being a journey. This apparent appearance is all to reinforce the idea that there's something happening. Karma and destiny and reincarnation are just part of that illusory idea that there's someone there who can act and have to pay for that. There isn't anyone there.

So looking at it completely round the other way, there is no one, so there can't be anything like karma. Except in the mind. Who's going to reincarnate? And there is no need to reincarnate, because when that apparent body/mind dies there is simply joy without cause. That's what you are. You are the joy that overflowed into this.

o   o   o

Tony, when you speak, sometimes I get this incredible sense of relief, enormous relief, and yet immediately, behind that, comes the fear and the 'Yes buts'.

Yes, I think I talked about an e-mail from a woman in America who said she'd read the book and she was really angry with me for giving her so much freedom, giving her total freedom – 'How dare you?'

I don't say that.

No, but she also said 'Isn't it crass for me to say that?' I didn't give her the freedom – she saw it. I'm not giving anybody anything. There isn't anyone here to give anyone there anything; there's no one there who needs anything given to them.

When I feel the fear – I've felt both, sitting here, within the last ten minutes – there's a helplessness about knowing that there is nothing I can do to stop that fear coming in and interfering with this ...

But the fear is the beloved.

As well?

Absolutely. There is nothing which is not the beloved. It's absolutely OK to feel anything, really. Everything is the beloved. Nothing is denied.

○　○　○

Don't we have a responsibility to that bit of ourselves that could say 'Who cares?' and be quite cruel to other people?

No, not at all. Cruelty is the beloved being cruel. Cruelty, genocide, not feeding the cat that night, watching *EastEnders* – it's all the divine expression. It has no meaning, and it's going nowhere. It's purposeless appearance. Who has the responsibility? Who is there? Even God doesn't have any responsibility, because God isn't going anywhere. God doesn't need to go anywhere because God is this.

Would you say that wanting to go home is denied if we are already there?

Absolutely. Seeking is the continual denial of home. It's the most effective way not to discover that home already is; I am already that. 'No I can't be – it must be over there. I've got to clear my chakras. I must go and see some master or other. I must still the mind. I must destroy the ego'. It's all nonsense; it's all saying this is not it.

What is the impulse for wanting to do things? 'I want to go here, I want to go there' – what is that impulse? I find myself analysing that, saying 'Oh, that's just the mind wanting to do this and that'.

If you take any activity to its end, you'll discover you are trying to come home. Any motivation – be it seemingly negative or positive – even the motivation of the victim is to find that they are the joy without cause. All motivation is only for that.

So does it ever serve any purpose to look at that wanting – not going with it but just observing it?

Observing what?

Observing the desire.

It's not about observing – it's about seeing. This is to do with words. For me, observation is a personal thing of the mind which looks at something and judges its value. Seeing is simply seeing what is, and that can be the desire, the longing for anything, the impulse. You can see the impulse to do anything; it can be seen.

Everything is seen. But if you also contemplate what's behind that impulse, you'll discover it's the longing to be what you already are.

You said it's an invitation. What allows the acceptance of that invitation?

The dropping of the illusion of 'me'. Then it's discovered that there is no invitation. The invitation is only there as long as there's a sense that there's something separate, to need to pick up the card. Once the card's picked up it vanishes and there's nothing. And that is the dropping of the illusion that there's someone there who needs to pick the card up. But there's nothing *you* can do about that; you can't pick the card up. But you already know that.

There's so much happening in this room that it doesn't matter anymore. Something in there hears this, something in there knows this. Once that's even opened to for a moment then your head is in the tiger's mouth – that's it.

o   o   o

Tony, when you talk about the presence, is that an illusion too? There isn't a presence?

Well, there is only no thing, out of which everything arises. When there is no one and there is only presence, then you can come and tell me that it certainly wasn't illusory, it isn't illusory. The joy without cause is the only thing that isn't illusory. It's the only constant. Being is the only constant, presence is the only constant. Everything else arises out of that. Without presence, there can be nothing.

What about recognition? The word 'recognition' came to my mind you recognise the presence.

Yes, you remember, there is a recognition of what you already are. That's it. It's directly behind you now – it's just back there, watching you watching me. You are the one that sees that looking at this. It's silence, it's stillness, it's no thing. It's not recognisable; you can't name it. It simply is there. And following initial recognition there is a merging and no longer a this and that.

o   o   o

Tony, what is the mechanism that obscures the seeing? I woke up a few weeks ago, half in, half out of a dream, bird sounds outside … Except they weren't outside; they were definitely coming from within me. Then everything from that moment – the sheets on my skin, smells, a dog barking, whatever – it was all coming from within me. It was definitely from no place; it was from the centre. Then there seemed to be a mind going, 'Wow, this is really cool! This is what he's on about in those books and those meetings'.

The mechanism is that oneness uses the mind to regurgitate the dream, to make the dream happen, the dream 'Wow! This is happening to Jonathan', if you like, in simple terms. 'For the last five minutes Jonathan hasn't been here. Isn't that wonderful? Now, what did we do? What did you do, Jonathan?' The mind will go back into the dream, into the game of 'There is such a thing as time, this happened to Jonathan, so he must be getting somewhere'.

It just so happened when this body/mind wasn't anymore, walking across the park, and there was oneness, it also so happened that a whole lot of clarity jumped in at the same time. And it does for a lot of people. It just depends on where you are with that and what happens.

No reason for the clarity then.

No, except that in the end we all know this, we all know it's all right for this to jump in and then jump out again. It is all the divine game – jumping in, jumping out … In a way behind your question is, 'Is there something wrong with the event of the mind coming in and saying what it says?' There's nothing wrong with that, because that's consciousness playing the mind coming in and saying to Jonathan, 'Five minutes ago you were being'.

Is that less likely to happen each time?

The more there's a clarity that everything is the divine expression, the less heat there is around there being one state that's better than another. There *is* no state that's better than another, because this is the game.

So that was a state for Jonathan?

Well no, actually – beingness is not a state. The mind thinks it is, so it thinks that the state of beingness is better than the state of not-being. It's bullshit – they are all one.

So does the clarity improve? If there are glimpses, does the clarity show itself a bit more each time?

It can do, yes.

Would you say that there are different levels of awareness?

No.

Well, if that's not the case … We have six billion people on earth and they're all aware.

No we don't – we have six billion *apparent* people.

OK, apparent people, and they're all apparently aware …

No they aren't. There is awareness and there are apparently six billion people in the world, a lot of whom think they are people, and awareness is overlaid by that sense of 'me'. However, everyone is being and thinks they are 'me-ing'.

OK, you have awareness, but you don't have general levels of clarity which would lead to liberation. Why is that?

But they do, because those apparent people don't exist anyway. They are an illusory appearance in a mind/body and, when it dies, awareness or joy without cause is simply there. So everybody is awakened. The people you think don't reach enlightenment already are, and when the body/mind dies, it's simply the end of the illusion, and there is joy.

o   o   o

You say that when the body/mind dies there is joy but that's just a concept. None of us knows what happens when we die.

I do, because I am already that. And so are you. It's only the mind that thinks it doesn't know.

The point I'm making is that to be able to be aware to a level which leads to clarity, which leads to liberation, awareness has to be very very deep.

Being simply is, and you are that. It has nothing to do with great depth or great sacrifice or great intelligence. You are already that.

Theoretically, yes, but …

No, you are already that. You know that you are the one that sees that you are joy without cause.

Well, I don't feel that at the moment!

No, that's OK! That's oneness not thinking it knows that it is joy without cause – join the club.

o   o   o

Tony, traditional teachers tell us that one of the barriers to awareness is the runaway mind going into the past and into the future. Eckhart Tolle, for example. I think that's most people's experience, but you don't talk about that. And when you say the mind, do you mean the thinking, it's the thinking that is a barrier because it's not accepting?

There is no barrier. The mind is only a collection of thoughts, and thoughts are not the barrier. Nothing is the barrier – except the idea that there is a barrier. And even that is an invitation.

When the thoughts are living with incidents from twenty years ago or what might happen in ten years, aren't they a barrier?

No, they're just thoughts about what might happen in ten years' time.

They're not carrying one away from the present?

They are just thoughts. You can't be carried away from this you *are* this, and what arises in this is the thought about what's going to happen in ten years' time.

It's really very different to other teachers.

It is totally different. Let's be very clear about this – that sort of teaching comes from the misunderstanding that there is someone there who thinks, and that thinking takes them away from what they are. There *is* no one there, and there is also no one there who can choose to think or not to think. There is simply no one; there is only being. And anything can arise in that being, including the thought of what's going to happen in ten years' time.

The trouble with the mind is that it's very tricky, and the guru mind will convince people – and it's a fascinating idea – that thoughts are like the devil. Thoughts are oneness, thought-ing.

It's interesting because it seemed to be that Eckhart Tolle woke up because he went almost crazy – but then in his book he's giving a description of how you can wake up which has nothing to do with that.

He's giving a method, a method of sensing inside the body.

It's a dualistic teaching – it's a teaching about the idea that there is someone there who can do something about not being there.

There is no 'I am aware' in awareness.

No, there is just being.

o   o   o

Earlier you spoke about the unique individual. How do you reconcile that with no one being there?

The unique individual is the appearance; there is the appearance of a unique individual. And that's very powerful – you know, that wall is your wall. But what's happening in the whole of that appearance is only the invitation. So the unique individual, with apparently thirty-five years of uniquely living like this and that and that and that *(points to people in audience)*, is only actually the beloved living in the invitation to discover that it is the beloved, living in the sense of separation. All these different apparent situations are actually only singular appearances, and all of them are the invitation.

See, it's very powerful in a way, because the whole thing about being a unique individual – or what seems to be a unique individual – goes on strengthening the hypnotic dream that we all have separate lives we're leading which have a meaning. And so we go on looking for this meaning – 'I'm going to find the meaning of my life'. And the invitation of that is to go on searching for this meaning until we give up.

And then when there's a giving up, there is the possibility that the idea that there's anyone there is also given up. It's the great and wonderful paradox …

Amsterdam
April 2002

There's an old friend of mine – we'd been friends since we went to school together quite a few years ago, we'd been friends all our lives. There was always a close connection, even though sometimes we didn't see each other for a few years. We had the sort of friendship that doesn't have any agenda. We were able to talk to each other in a way which we wouldn't necessarily share with other people. Fairly recently, he died.

One afternoon, a few weeks before his death, I went to see him. We sat there and had a cup of tea, and there was something going on with this guy. He was so angry. He was a very lovely and happy guy in many ways, but that afternoon he was angry. At that last meeting he knew somewhere he was going to die. He hadn't been told that, but somewhere inside he knew. He needed to express anger and resentment and he did.

I went back to Claire and I said to her, 'What's going on with him?' A month later he was dead.

He'd known a lot of famous people, and at his memorial service many people made speeches about him. At the end of it all, my friend was a saint, a total saint, without any vestige of anger or judgement about anyone.

All I'm really telling you this for is to illustrate the way we always want to create heroes. The mind loves the idea of heroes. The people in the audience wanted to turn this man into a saint who loved everybody and was always forgiving and caring.

Last night we were talking about Ramana Maharshi and

Nisargadatta and all these beautiful people because also, in the search for enlightenment, the mind creates heroes. And the wonderfully clever thing about creating heroes is that you can always be sure that you can never be like them. The people who create heroes go on living in this mental circuit of 'This man is really astounding! I can never be like that. I don't actually have to become awake'.

The creation of heroes is one way the mind avoids awakening. There will always be figures who are great spiritual heroes. The guy who decides to teach and become a master starts to talk to a few people, who then make him into a hero. They tell other people about this great hero and the other people come along too … And everybody is projecting on to everyone else. The disciples are making this teacher up, and in doing so, they're making their own position up too. The terminology they use is amazing. People come to me and say, 'I have just been to a great master'.

Master/disciple – it's the whole mind-set. We go on reinforcing the idea of 'I am under/you are above'. Basically, as far as I'm concerned, it's all about avoidance. We want a daddy or a mummy who is going to do it for us because we don't think we can do it ourselves. (Of course, the other problem is that we think there is something that can be done …) It's all a mind-game – the mind creates this figure which we then become devoted to and sit under in order for awakening to emerge.

The sea-change that I see happening is that some people who are communicating this are just doing so as friends. They are ordinary people who are friends. It's much more difficult to project that heroism on to them.

The other thing that I think people are realising is that the person who is communicating this doesn't have anything they don't.

There is no one here who has anything more. In fact, actually this is about having nothing. A lot of people who come to these meetings are rich – rich with concepts. Awakening is about being without anything.

You are suggesting that there is a way to avoid awakening. But if there is no way to make awakening happen, surely there can't be any way to avoid it either?

No, absolutely. There is no one who avoids, but avoidance arises, I've noticed. I'm not suggesting for a moment that anybody can do anything about this, because the whole crux of what is being said here is that there is no choice, that there is no one.

Are there just differences in levels of communication of the state of awakeness, or are there different levels of enlightenment?

No, there are no levels of enlightenment. There is just seeing and not seeing. There is absolute unicity, or there is apparent separation.

So in this enlightened state, we're not resisting anything which arises – neuroses, preferences, anger – and we're just sitting watching this happen and that happen and that happen ...

No, none of that. First of all, this is not a state. There isn't anybody who's watching or not watching, and there isn't anybody who's accepting or not accepting. There simply is what is arising. And in that what-is-arising, there can be anger, resistance or anything you'd like to name, but there is no longer anyone here. I am this, and in this there can be resistance, anger, ego, all sorts, which arise. That's what arises and that is celebrated. There isn't anybody doing anything.

But initially, as you said earlier, there's a watching of this.

Initially, yes, there is still apparently a dancing in and out, and there are things happening over here and things happening over there. Or things happening over here and nothing happening over there. And all that happens is the balance changes, and the being apparently takes over from the 'me'-ing.

It's just that earlier you talked about the establishment of it, and I thought that if one were going to do anything at all ... I've found it really helpful to put my attention on the awareness rather than on the imaginings of the mind.

That's fine. That's the way it is for that body/mind. That's not a general recommendation, though – that's just how it is for that body/mind (although there is no one choosing that). It might be for that body/mind that meditation in some form or other might arise. But that doesn't mean to say, 'Let's all meditate'. It's just that that's how it works in your case; that's how it's opening. I say to some people, 'Become very intimate with this'. For some people that rings a bell somewhere and they do open to being intimate with being or with this. For other people, this simply doesn't resonate.

There's a nice little metaphor arising in this awareness, and that is that in a way you are a sort of horse-whisperer. The mind is whispering continuously, 'This is me who's going to get you somewhere. We're going to undertake some big project now ...' There is a continual whispering. And then we meet a horse-whisperer, in the form of Tony Parsons, who is contra-whispering, saying constantly, 'This whispering is ...' Now I'm stuck!

It's not contra, actually – it's beyond contra. The whispering goes into a big hole.

Yes, of course – you push the whispering into a big hole.

No, I don't – I don't do anything. There isn't anybody here doing anything. There's no agenda here, there is absolutely no agenda. There's nothing here.

o   o   o

You know when you said there is no evolution, are you saying that in the context of this room of appearances there isn't evolution?

There only appears to be evolution – it's only another appearance. It's to convince you that things are going somewhere. And if things are going somewhere, then you can go somewhere. 'Come on,' the mind says, 'I'll take you there. What this guy Tony Parsons is talking about is very good. If we get together, you and I, I can get you there – next week … Or maybe next year'.

The world's evolution is a wonderful play to convince us that there is the journey. There isn't. It's a play, it's a film, a film called 'The World'. The film looks as though it's going somewhere. You're in a film and you're the main character and we're all the characters that support that film star. That's how it appears.

And if you stop the film, there's just one thing after another.

There's just one thing.

Could you say we're the screen on which the film is projected?

You are the light that allows the film to be. And if you see it all from another point of view, you begin to open up to the possibility of dropping the idea of a journey towards somewhere that you'll never get to. You'll never get there – you already are there. And so in a way, the film is sacred. It's telling you that you are that. I want to get you out of the idea – or rather I don't, but something wants to get you out of the idea that you're on a journey.

When there is simply presence, all meaning ends. Meaning is always attached to a story – 'We are going somewhere'.

o   o   o

You said on your tape something about recognising that life is deep disappointment and then you can relax, because you're not going to try and make things work. But life isn't always deep disappointment.

Oh no, no, no.

Did you mean, well, it's always going to be disappointing in the end so don't bother?

Oh no, the one who is still thinking that they're living in the film will generally believe – most times, not always – that it's going to work out in the end.

But it doesn't stop you from fully participating.

After awakening, for the first time you participate; before that you're always trying to get somewhere. You're in business, you're in a deal. Seekers are always in a deal – finders give up dealing. Finders give up the deal, give up everything for this. And everything is the journey of time, the idea that you can get it next week …

Just give up – this is it. Isn't it wonderful, to give up that agonising bloody journey, and that target your mum and dad said you should get to? Just forget it. You're there.

It's just a recognition of that fact.

And to the mind, it's frightening. We're talking about the unknown. 'What's this guy talking about, giving up everything? I've got a house and a wife and three mistresses – am I going to give them all up?' It's frightening. 'What's he saying? Stop! This is all there is? This is it?'

'It's more difficult for a rich man to enter the kingdom of heaven'. The richness has nothing to do with money – it's got to do with concepts. All you give up is the idea of 'me'. And it can seem like everything.

And these concepts seem to promise that I'll be safe; without them, I feel quite unsafe.

Oh very. Mind you, you never have been safe actually, but you think you have. Let go of that and you let go of everything. 'What does it profit a man that he gains the world and suffers the loss of his soul?' There is no soul, but this is about total and utter poverty.

The kingdom of heaven is like a pearl in the field, and the farmer gives up everything for that. We have to give up absolutely everything for this – everything. But we can't do it! So that's a relief, isn't it! But somewhere we know that, and when that's opened to, then it can happen.

And to the mind, that's really frightening because everything falls away. Everything that you think you are falls away – time, deals ... all fall away. There is just this. So you are left with absolutely nothing. And you have absolutely everything. Because you are absolutely everything. It's very simple!

o   o   o

This system is much more relaxing, to go for the ordinary rather than to go for the amazing.

You're describing how it is for you. And I'm the same, actually – I love the ordinariness of it. It's very gently ordinary. And yet there is a magnificence about it ... Claire describes it as a gentle wow.

In fact, there's nothing to be frightened of – there really is nothing, you couldn't be in a safer place. It's the only security there is. Presence is the only secure constant.

Whenever I look anywhere, it has a relation to 'What can I get out of it?' or it has a relation to a 'me' who wants something. So I never see the actual essence of what is.

No, of course not, because you're living in the deal, you're living in business, so everything you see is business.

Does it matter whether you think you want this or not?

No, not at all. Let's be clear about this – this has nothing to do with you. It has nothing to do with the way you should be wanting it, not wanting it …

There are people who teach that unless you are absolutely serious, deeply serious and sincere about this, it'll never happen. There are other people who say, if you're honest inside, if you have an honest longing to give up everything for this, it'll happen … It's the list, it's the usual mind-game. 'You've got to be like that before you can get your exam results'. All of these teachings spring straight from the guru-mind which is rooted in a deep and abiding ignorance about the nature of the absolute.

This is the divine expression. What this is – right at this moment – is it. Just sit there and be life.

It's just that I had a reaction that I didn't *want it, when I arrived here.*

Well, I'll tell you something surprising – not wanting it is getting very close. Really! There is somebody who says you won't get it unless you long for it, and then there's somebody else, in Bombay, who says, 'If you don't care and you give up the whole idea of it, then it's available'. So who believes who? The mind can go mad with all this, working out all the different possibilities. All that's happening here right now is that you're sitting on a chair. That's all there is. There is only this. It's so utterly simple.

Is there any benefit in knowing that?

There is a benefit in having some clarity, yes. It's good to be clear about this. If there's clarity, then everything falls out of the way for there just to be this. So you could say, yes, there is a benefit, but it's a benefit to no one.

o   o   o

One of the things I think that's difficult with this sense of there just being things happening is this feeling of the person. The difficult bit to allow just to happen is the person that you think you are. We're so used to this person we carry around with us – we think he's real. So when we come across the possibility that this character is just another thing that's happening, that can be difficult.

So many people say to me, 'Well I'm still here – there's still a "me" '. There is a character; there is, if you like, a personality.

Words are difficult – for some people the word 'personality' still seems to be tied up with the ego. But there is a personality – Tony Parsons has certain characteristics and acts in a certain way. That's absolutely fine, that's just another thing that's apparently happening; there's no question that Tony Parsons is happening. But so is the car that's just going by, and so is the sunshine. Those things are also just happening, and there's no one there that they're happening to. It's as simple that. Of course, it is all appearance.

So give yourself permission for that to be a bit of a confusion; for that still to be something that is just going to emerge.

Go on feeling that whatever's felt in the body or whatever thoughts arise are absolutely fine. There's nothing wrong with thinking. There's nothing wrong with time-thinking, with planning, with worrying, with feeling fear – with feeling anything. Just begin to try and let that just be there on its own, as something that's happening, without any sense of judgement, without trying to look for any sort of meaning at all. Just forget about looking for meaning, and let what's happening just be there, the feelings, the thoughts … Even the pushing away or the resistance to what's happening is, again, something that's just happening.

I'm sure a lot of people here have a sense of being. For many people, the more they're in this sort of openness, the more that sense of being is there, and it's very sweet. People often say to me, 'But then it goes away, because I contract'. Actually, it doesn't go away–what happens is a sense of contraction arises. Being is all there is, and the sense of contraction, the sense of 'me', arises in presence.

It's wonderful when you can enjoy your personality, but when you don't enjoy it it's not so wonderful!

I know, but what doesn't enjoy it? What doesn't enjoy it is the ego that wants to get something–like becoming a pure Tony Parsons, God forbid! The ego thinks that the character, the person, should become worthy. And the crazy thing is that it never will become worthy because it doesn't need to be worthy, because it is already divine.

In presence what you are is divine–including all the things that the mind thinks are neurotic or unworthy. Those things are divine. All those knobbly bits are divine and can be there forever. It just so happens that once there is an opening to what you are, then those neurotic things tend to go to sleep, to fade away. They don't have the same power that they did. However, that is a secondary occurrence.

But what we are discussing has nothing to do with becoming anything or being worthy. What you are, right now, is perfectly appropriate ... the divine play.

And as I've said before, another thing that emerges is that once your self is embraced by what you are, then of course there's an embracing of what other people appear to be. When Christ came on earth, he said, 'I do away with the Ten Commandments and give you two–love God and love thy neighbour'. Well, in his day, he had to speak like that. What he really meant was 'See there is only oneness and then everything else follows from that' including loving this, which is loving that, loving your neighbour as yourself. Because in the end, what I see when I see Bill is myself. All you're seeing is yourself.

But that follows. There's nothing you can do; you can't make that happen. It just follows naturally out of that clear seeing.

I sometimes tell myself, 'There must be some very stubborn unworthiness in you in that you haven't made use of the gifts you've been given in the right way. You could have made much better use of them'.

Everything that has apparently happened in your life is absolutely perfectly appropriate. Not one thing could have been any different. That's the way it had to be. If, for instance, in your work, you look back and say, 'With that person, I could have done better', actually that person needed exactly what happened – not another thing that seemed, to the mind, to be better – as the absolute invitation for them. The invitation is present and being re-created all of the time, and when it seems as if somebody apparently behaves against a person or could have 'done better' with them, in fact what happened at the time was totally appropriate.

Unworthiness is something we grow up with – that's part of the drama. We grow up, most of us, feeling unworthy about being able to deal with the world, and feeling unworthy in ourselves in comparison with the perfect images we project. Even in the ordinary world we have all these images of other people who seem to be better than us. And when we come to this sort of thing, of course, we feel even more unworthy. We look at people like Ramana Maharshi and say, 'Well, I can never be like that'.

It's all a way of avoiding the actual reality, and that is that what we are is beyond who we think we are or are not. There is no way that anybody has to be more intelligent, more sensitive … What you are is the one, the absolute, the presence, the immaculate conception.

You just said that things are perfectly appropriate, but to whom?

To no one. It's not perfectly appropriate to the mind – the mind will never find anything that's perfectly appropriate. Because the mind is always trying to get somewhere; there's always somewhere that the mind wants to get to. It lives in division, it lives in time. So in the world we see what seems to be division, and we live in that division of worthiness or unworthiness, or good or bad, or whatever you like. This is the immaculate conception appearing as the immaculate misconception. But as far as presence is concerned, everything is what it is.

It's appropriate to what you are, rather than who you are; or who you think you are. Because in the end, you see, nothing is going anywhere. Nothing has ever gone anywhere and nothing is going anywhere now. There is simply this. So nothing has to be different or become anything. No one has to be different or become anything. This is it.

o   o   o

Can I ask a question about the thinking process? I found this morning and particularly last night when I was in bed that my mind got completely immobilised by trying to work all this out. Last night particularly, it came to a complete stop.

That's the idea of this! This is all about the immobilising of the mind, the setting of the mind on one side. What we're doing here is setting the mind on one side for it simply to perform its natural function – which is to work out things like, for instance, the best way to fly to America. Here we're putting the mind in its natural place. And it seems a bit frightening or alarming because the mind can't get anywhere. The mind will never get anywhere with this. It will just function naturally.

I think that when the mind looks at this utter simplicity it meets a brick wall, and there is a feeling of discomfort about that. In a way the mind is meeting a brick wall all the time here. The mind keeps thinking 'Yes, but what about -?' and keeps on coming up against this brick wall.

It gives us nothing to hang on to.

No, there isn't anything.

That's what's the uncomfortable part of it. Normally, I'd like to think I think logically – if I do this, then something happens; and if I do that, then something else happens. But it isn't like that.

No, there's no result.

And you can even think about not thinking about it, and the same thing happens in reverse. There just isn't anything to get a grip on.

No, there's no result. There will never be a continuation here. This is about nothing. And really, when that's going on, what then can happen is suddenly there is simply this – sitting on a chair. For a lot of people, there's a lot of talk goes on and mind-stuff goes on – just drop it and all that's happening is sitting on a chair. And there you are – there is this. Just rest in this. Forget all the words and the logic. Keep on coming back to this.

All that's happening is that the beloved is simply saying 'Come back'. This is what this is all about – 'Just come back, come back'. 'Oh yeah, but what about -?' 'Yeah, OK – come back, come back'. This is just about coming home.

o   o   o

When I'm with someone who's very shy, for example, and I say 'What's the difference between him and me?', I realise that there is in fact no difference – except that he thinks he should be shy; there's something dangerous about not being shy. I can see there's no difference in a way – it's just an idea. Now if I relate that to awakening, it's probably just an idea that's obstructing it.

Oh, totally. It's the 'I' thought playing a particular game to protect itself.

But still I don't see that it is just the idea.

The idea that you are a person is something that was adopted when you were a kid, and since then you've gone on reinforcing the idea until you take it really seriously. You take seriously that original idea that you are separate and that you are an individual. You've spent years building up a very strong belief in your existence. There's such huge investment in the person you think you are; you think that's the real thing. You take seriously the idea of the person and for years and years you've maintained and created a life that sustains that person and serves that person. (It doesn't actually, but that's what's been going on.) For years and years you've protected that person and tried to satisfy the needs of that person.

And there's a belief that if that person isn't there, then that's the end of everything. The great fear is that if the person isn't there, then everything will end. And the other fear that arises, I think for some people, is that if that person isn't there they will lose their mind and become unbalanced. Certainly, for most people it's losing that which is in a way most precious – the sense of 'me'.

Awakening doesn't come down to you – there is simply light. The apparent darkness that overlays the light is the idea that there's a person there, which has been reinforced during what seems like a process of years. But that feeling of there being a person can drop away instantaneously. It does every night anyway, but it can drop away in your conscious day just like that.

And that is what awakening is – the realisation that there is no one to awaken. Liberation arises when it's discovered that there is no one to liberate.

I have a difficulty with imagining the no one.

You can't. You who are apparently someone can't imagine the no one – it's impossible. The only thing I ever really in the end say (apart from 'All there is is this') is, 'Try in some way to be open to the possibility and the sense that whatever is moving is simply a movement'. To put it another way, whatever is happening is simply happening, and it's happening to no one. It's utterly, utterly simple. In other words, instead of there being a person there, let there be nothing there but what is.

There is just activity and you associate that with a person called Bill or whatever. But all there actually is is activity. And there's no way I can make anybody see this and there's no way you can make it happen. But it's happening – it's happening here and it's happening elsewhere.

You've had it now – you're lost. You should never have come here! I can tell you it's going to happen. And it could happen in five minutes' time, in terms of the way the mind thinks of time. There's no question that it can happen because it's happening all the time, the dropping away of the sense of there being anyone. It's infectious.

You don't have to believe it, you don't even have to understand it. It's so simple, it doesn't need understanding. Just see that there is activity. Let there be the seeing of activity. Everybody in this room is actually doing it – the only thing that's happening in this room is the seeing of activity. But in some way or other there's an idea that there's a 'you' seeing it and 'you' are doing it or it is being done to 'you'.

Most people think this is about something very special. A lot of people think they can come to something like this and find something special which will then make them somehow stand out in a crowd. People will come up to them and say, 'I hear you're enlightened. Would you mind coming round to see some of my friends?' And you go round and see the friends, and next time you go round there are more friends, there are quite a lot of people and they can't see you very easily, so you say to your friend, 'Let's go to a group room – it's bigger'. You go there and there are now sixty-five people there. And still it's a bit difficult for them to see you, so you have a platform built … It's the enlightenment game.

Two Catholic priests were praying at the altar when suddenly one of them stood up and passionately exclaimed, 'Oh Lord, I am nothing compared to your glory! See I am nothing!' The other priest was also inspired to rise to his feet, saying 'I am nothing! I am nothing!'

A cleaner sweeping the floor at the back of the church was so moved by the scene that he too began crying out, 'I am nothing, Lord! I am nothing!'

Whereupon one priest turned to the other and said, 'Who does he think he is, claiming to be nothing?'

Amsterdam
July 2002

People come here with the idea that if they listen to the words, if they succeed in understanding the nature of what they are, they can then fall into that. But it doesn't work like that, because the nature of what we are is totally beyond understanding. In fact, it is understanding that falls away before clear seeing happens. Clear seeing has nothing to do with understanding.

The only thing that can happen here, in terms of understanding, is the dropping of the ideas you have about enlightenment, about what you think you are. The ideas can drop away and you can be left with no idea, with nothing. And when you're left with nothing, what emerges is *this*. What emerges is the invitation. All of the sensory messages that you're getting touching, smelling, seeing – are all the lover inviting you to see that there is only oneness.

It is utterly simple and totally immediate. You are sitting in what you are. In fact, you are what is.

And it has nothing to do with who you think you are. You are just a character in a play. The play is not going to change – nothing is going to get better or worse – but what emerges is the one that sees. Clear seeing is simply seeing without anyone being there.

All the time we are looking from the point of view of the separate being, we don't see what is really there; we see through a veil. Somewhere we are still trying to get something out of what we see – we look and hear in order to get something back. In clear seeing there is no one there who wants anything, and so what is seen is the reality. The reality is that there is only oneness.

You can't drop 'you'. There is no one there – there has never been anyone there who could drop or choose anything, so there is nothing that can be done. But there is something, just behind you, looking at you sitting here looking at me. What is seen is the character that has never needed to become anything better, that is totally and absolutely perfect in the play. That doesn't need to change for this clarity to happen; it can't change. There is no question of you having to change in order for liberation to happen. Liberation has nothing to do with you.

Everybody in the world for whom awakening hasn't happened feels alienated. Whether there is a war going on, or whether you live in a beautiful penthouse in New York ... all the time there is a sense of separation there is something missing. After awakening, that apparent life story still goes on but the identification with it is totally lost.

So basically we are spectators in our own soap?

Yes, in a way, except that it even goes beyond that. There is no spectator here anymore of the soap called 'Tony Parsons'. There is just oneness, and Tony Parsons arises in that. Just like this glass does. At first, when people open to this, there can be a sense of a watcher of the drama. That falls away.

Tony, can there be a full realisation of not-knowing when there is still the belief in the 'me' present?

No. All belief falls away. Belief is related to a 'me'.

So a state of not-knowing is not compatible with a 'me'?

It isn't. But the difficulty is that the mind falls into the trap of thinking in terms of a permanence in which awakening exists and there is no longer any 'me'-ing. The mind wants to think that after awakening, there is no possibility of a sense of 'me'. But that isn't the reality. Oneness has nothing to do with time. If there is the idea that the 'me' should never emerge again, then there is another imprisonment – the imprisonment of there never being a 'me' arising.

Another difficulty with the mind is it tends to personalise awakening. Oneness has nothing to do with anyone and totally embraces all that appears, including ego and belief.

And knowing?

And knowing. Liberation denies nothing. Knowledge and ego are oneness ego-ing and knowledge-ing. All of it is the dance happening. It is all the one, playing the game of two.

o   o   o

What if the character in this oneness is unhappy? Is therapy useful?

This is the difficulty with words. There is no character that is unhappy anymore – there is simply oneness, and in oneness unhappiness can arise. But there is no longer any identification with a person who is unhappy, so there is no reason to try to change that. There is no question of ever needing to change anything anymore but, of course, apparent change can arise.

So what to do with pain?

Just see that there is pain arising. But not for anyone awakening is the dropping of the one who owns anything. It is simply the seeing of life happening – including pain, joy … anything. What I am embraces that, without any sense that it needs to be changed.

So all you can say is 'feel the pain'?

No, the moment you say that, you are back into the idea that there is a person who can feel it. Strangely enough, we are living in the paradise, but it is not the mind's picture of what paradise is. It is a total freedom and acceptance of everything that is, without any sense that it needs to be changed.

Nobody here *(points to self)* embraces anything. Oneness doesn't embrace anything because oneness doesn't need to. Oneness is everything. Oneness is all there is. And in all there is can arise a headache. But oneness doesn't then say, 'Oh, there is a headache – I will embrace it!' Oneness is headache-ing.

Liberation isn't liberation if it can't embrace and accept non-liberation. The concept we have about enlightenment is just another prison constructed by the mind.

But isn't it possible that some people would need to clean out their personality?

The mind would think so, yes.

I feel there are some things in myself I need to look at, otherwise I don't even know that they're there but they'd still wield their influence. It makes me feel better and freer when I pay attention to certain parts of 'me'.

It is absolutely fine to look at your life and to feel better about it. But all you end up with is someone who feels better about their life because they have looked at it. This has no relationship or relevance to oneness.

I have the feeling that, doing this, some steps have been taken.

Steps can be taken, but there is no step that can be taken to that which already is. It isn't over there – there *is* only oneness. You can't creep up on what already is.

o   o   o

How do you know that you are awakened?

You don't.

But you say that you are in oneness …

No, I'm not *in* oneness – there is oneness.

You don't know what enlightenment is?

I couldn't put it into words. There is no way that anyone needs to know what oneness is, because oneness is the natural state.

Oneness is all there is. It's like saying, 'So you don't know when the sun shines'.

Why does Tony Parsons want to say all this?

Tony Parsons doesn't want to say all this. In some way or other, one – which plays the game of two – is playing the game of rediscovery; that is the drama. The drama is that there is only oneness that manifests as twoness. It thinks it has lost itself and wants to find itself again, so it goes to see Tony Parsons. Communication happens so that the invitation is seen, and oneness is then there again.

So you want us to see that?

No I don't.

Why do you communicate this?

I don't. Communication is happening.

o o o

Being here now, and what you said in the beginning about the invitation coming through the senses – isn't that similar?

It seems to be, yes. But the whole teaching of being here now is communicated to an apparent person who has choice. The teaching about the dropping of thought and seeing thought as a disease – all of that is based on the erroneous premise that there is someone who can choose. There isn't – there is no one.

The idea that we live in total being or total invitation all the time transcends the idea that anybody can do anything about that. I haven't suggested for a moment that you go into your body and feel your senses, or that you try through touch to become intimate with something, because there is no one here who can do it. But in some very direct way, the wisdom that is there knows this. What happens is that the mind which is overlaying that falls away, and there is just a sense of is-ness.

Hearing and smelling and all that is in the now.

As far as I'm concerned, there is no such thing as now. 'Now' implies that there is a then – you're back in time. 'Now' is this moment – but there *is* no moment. There is only this. It's timeless. It isn't now and it wasn't then. There is an abyss between the two concepts.

People who adopt this idea of being in the now hear this message and they rush around 'being in the now' for at least three days, and then it all falls apart. There is a lovely cartoon of a girl looking in the mirror and saying, 'Well, tomorrow morning I'm going to start being here now again'. It's another formula.

So all one can do is wake up out of that and not invest in that?

Well, that is another sort of doing. There is no one there who can choose that. If you go on hearing that there is no one there and nothing can be done, then something else can start to happen. The last bit of the jigsaw can suddenly drop into place.

Is it the case that when you don't do anything life leads you to awakening?

It is not leading you to awakening – there is no way that you can be led to what already is.

But if you don't see it and you don't do anything anymore – then what?

Well, what can possibly happen is that you reach somewhere called nothing; you're left with nothing. It's very dangerous to listen to this, because what you are led to is nothing. There is nothing to do, there is nowhere to go. When there is nothing, it is possible that this is seen.

I used to be someone who would really go for all sorts of different things but now it doesn't happen anymore, and I get desperate with boredom sometimes. It feels terrible.

For some people, in awakening, there can be periods of flatness, of dryness.

I didn't realise till now that boredom could somehow be a plus.

Well, in a way, the desert – or boredom happening – is a sign that there is a giving up.

o　o　o

I know this oneness – it happened twenty years ago, and again five years ago for a whole week.

It's never stopped happening – it is the only thing there is. But the sense of 'me' emerges again, and the problem is that we think that the 'me' coming in again is somehow wrong. Actually, the emergence of 'me' is absolutely perfect – the 'me' needs to come back. It is all part of the process of seeing that 'me' coming in is just what is arising. It is not that 'me' coming in has pushed oneness out – what has happened in fact is that one has come back as 'me'. 'Me' is oneness, 'me'-ing. The mind is always dividing everything into two. 'I glimpsed oneness and then the ego came back' – as if those are two separate things.

o　o　o

Can you say something about choice? The other day I suddenly chose to go into the dining room and the curtain was on fire and the cat was in the room and could have been killed. What's that all about?

116

Choice is an appearance. At times it can be very convincing that there is something which is directing you to take an action, like putting something right in a room which was wrong. But actually what was wrong in the room? Where is this right or wrong? It's all in the mind, this idea that something was wrong which you were led to put right. If you had stayed in the other room, that is still simply what is arising. The curtains catching fire ... the cat being killed ... that is what is.

But the whole choice thing is very powerful, and we are continually living in this sense that we do make choices and that they lead to something. In a way we are avoiding our own nature all the time. We are always making up this little 'me' that lives in this thing called a life, just in order to avoid the discovery that we are the one. The discovery that there is only oneness is very frightening to a 'me'. 'Me' doesn't want that – it wants to keep its cat alive and it wants to be enlightened, which it believes is everything being OK. The mind doesn't want there to be a discovery of oneness – that's really frightening.

I'm still confused about choice. When the character Tony Parsons takes an aspirin because he has a headache, then that's not a choice but just something happening?

Nobody ever chooses anything. If you really look at what you think you chose last night or this morning, you'll discover that you didn't choose it. It was apparently chosen through you. There is no one there who chooses. It is all only an appearance of choice.

So we cannot help being here?

No. In the end there is no choice at any level. There isn't a God choosing, there isn't a God directing you – there isn't anything directing you. Nothing is chosen. There is only this.

So if everything still arises in Tony Parsons, does that also include the denial of oneness?

That can arise. It would be very difficult for that to arise now, because the source of everything can't be denied. It's got nothing to do with belief or doubt – there is simply oneness.

○   ○   ○

Does intuition stem from the mind?

No, I think it comes from the wisdom that is there. And I think this has a lot to do with intuition. You are never going to understand it or work it out – it's a leap, a sudden leap.

Is it not important that you lead a good life?

Oh God, no! The whole thing about leading a good life is just a conditioned idea of the mind. If you look at the different ways people recommend for 'leading a good life', they are very contrary. For some people, leading a good life is flying an aeroplane into the World Trade Center. It's ignorance; it's just the mind.

The whole of this appearance is merely a reflection of a longing to find that love which is totally beyond the concept of good or bad. The idea of goodness or badness is just a reflection of the real nature of things. The real nature of oneness is that it is unconditional love. It is a totally unassailable love without any sense of anything else. Our idea of good and bad is simply a very tepid reflection of that.

So it doesn't matter how you react to your children for example?

Nothing matters. What we are talking about here is totally beyond the individual and any sense of behaving – beyond being good, beyond being serious about enlightenment … all those things that some people tell you are so important. They are all locked into the idea of there being someone there who is or isn't a certain way.

All I can say is that the character that is there behaves in the way that the character does. It doesn't necessarily mean beating up the children. But if somebody does that, then that is oneness beating up oneness. And the whole of this appearance is kept in a total balance. Beating up children here is balanced by not beating up children there.

o o o

Is wisdom that you know the object because you are the object?

No, that's another sort of a formula. It is totally beyond anyone being the object and therefore knowing it. It is totally beyond any idea like that.

What is wisdom?

Well, wisdom is the nearest one can get to clarity, clear seeing. What is happening here is that clear seeing is communicating with clear seeing, which is hidden under the rubble of the mind. Clear seeing underneath is saying 'Yes!' The rubble of the mind is saying 'No!' or 'Yes but …'

So why is this whole show going on?

This is the eternal drama that one is playing. I am one appearing as two – including, in the appearance, the sense of separation – in order to discover that I am one.

My mind wants to know why.

Because it is wonderful to find out you're one after being two for a while. Go and bang your head against the wall and then stop. Really. It's as simple as that.

Why do we need to bang our heads?

It's fun – it's the game, it's the play. Actually you're not banging your head against the wall all the time really. You quite enjoy being two, don't you? Look how much you enjoy it. Obviously hardly anybody in this room wants oneness. There is a huge attachment to and fascination with being two looking for one. It's wonderful, it's divine, it's gorgeous – I love it! I go around Amsterdam seeing people really really holding on to their separation and their identity. They are all walking around trying really hard to be separate individuals. It's hugely fascinating!

o   o   o

Some people came to me because their son was taking drugs and they wanted my help. From what you say, the son taking drugs is just something that arises. But that does seem like taking an easy way out.

All the time that you identify with the situation, then there is always a 'me' who tries to change it or tries to change the way you communicate it. There is no agenda going on here – I don't have any investment in any of this. There is nobody here who has an investment in this, so there is no need to compromise what is being said here. And there is absolutely no desire to compromise it in order somehow to help people or please them. Because there is only oneness, there is nobody here trying to make other people one – because they are already one. There is no one here trying to help anybody. There is no help needed.

The greatest love is to share clarity and expose confusion. But there isn't anybody who shares that and there isn't anybody who has any investment in that. There is just clarity, clear seeing. What I am sees the appearance arising and knows that it is meaningless. To share this is compassion – to please the mind is manipulation. Of course, they are both simply what they are.

o   o   o

Has there been a change in the forcefulness of your communications? Do you get impatient with questions?

I don't know about forcefulness but over the years it seems that there is a much simpler communication going on. More direct and simple. But there's no impatience, because there is no one trying to get anywhere, there's nowhere to go. Every apparent question and apparent answer is totally unique and new ... It is what is.

o   o   o

It seems that it is the thought process that creates the 'me'.

'Me' is one, 'me'-ing. Everything is only one – there is nothing that isn't. Certainly the thought process is a tool that is very effectively used to reinforce the sense of 'me'. The mind is like a prism that the single light of the absolute shines through, and this turns the one light into a rainbow.

It's said that inattention breeds thinking, so it would seem that to try to be attentive ...

That is how the mind would see it, but who is it who is going to choose to be attentive? There isn't anyone. Inattention happens – inattention is the one being inattentive. The trouble with the mind is that it is always coming back to the presumption that there is someone who can choose to be a certain way that is better than another way. It is total ignorance, and most of our conditioning and most of the scriptures and even contemporary teachings speak from that point of view.

o   o   o

Sometimes, when you speak, I start nodding very firmly. I have a deep distrust of this nodding. I don't think it's nodding out of wisdom – it seems it's the outcome of a stubborn effort to understand.

It's nodding with an idea or a hope that understanding will arise?

Yes. I can't give up this tendency to try and understand.

It's difficult, because the idea of understanding something is very inviting. And also it takes you away from this – to have this wonderful task of understanding the nature of what I am takes me away from just this. 'I don't want to come back to life – I want to stay in the school of understanding'.

You will come to see that what is being communicated here is beyond the heart and mind of 'you'. This brings you to understand that there is nothing to understand.

Is there no way of using the mind to go in the other direction?

No, because the mind can only live in time. It denies the existence of no-time. It fights against the existence of no-time because in no-time – which is what we naturally are – it ceases sitting on the throne and running everything.

Where is the drive to eat food, to stay alive, coming from?

That is all part of the drama. The drama is eternal. It is substantiated by the sense of there being someone who can make their life work. That is how the drama continues, including finding food so that you don't starve. The drama will never end. The Twin Towers and Afghanistan will always go on, just with different names.

When you take this position – for example, about the 11th of September – a lot of people get very angry.

Yes, because this is a threat. Most people want their lives to be the most important thing in the world. But life is without purpose. That is its beauty.

They say that in the States 50,000 people are murdered every year.

Death is the celebration. Death is the putting out of the lamp because the dawn has broken. (I read that somewhere – good, isn't it?) Physical death is the seeing that there is only oneness, though that can happen before the physical body dies.

o o o

My mind is so bored …

It's always looking for something, isn't it? It's like the beggar who goes to the great emperor's gate with a bowl and says to the servants that he wants the emperor to try and fill his bowl. The emperor is in the garden and overhears the beggar. He goes over to him and says, 'This is ridiculous! I'm so rich – I'll fill it, no problem'. So he gets one of the servants to go and get jewellery, and as he puts it in the bowl, it vanishes. He gets some more jewellery and some gold, and he goes on and on, pouring his riches into the bowl, but they all vanish. In the end he is left with nothing.

He asks the beggar, 'How does this happen? What is this bowl?'

'The bowl', the beggar replies, 'is the mind'.

The mind is always looking for something more – 'What's going to happen next?' What we long for, we think we can get through the mind. So the mind is continually throwing up all sorts of riches and none of them ever satisfies. When you go and see people teaching about what is said to be the nature of enlightenment, the ones who teach some sort of process are still coming from the mind. It is very popular.

The nature of what we are is totally and utterly simple. It's here right now. It's this, the seeing of this. There is nothing complicated, there is nothing that needs to be done. But the mind wants the process of discovering our own nature to be complicated so that we don't find it. The mind wants to continue being employed. And it will go on and on and on forever. We go on filling the bowl with our mind's activity, and never ever will it be filled. Where did the idea of 27 levels of enlightenment come from?

The crazy thing about it is that what is being looked for is right in front of us. What we are looking for is what is right in this.

So what can one do with a bored mind?

Let there be the seeing of a bored mind. Who is actually telling me that the mind is bored? The seer is. So go back to the seer and just see whatever arises. It is not you seeing it – there is just seeing it. It's so simple, so immediate … That's it – that's what all the religions and all the scriptures are about – simply seeing this.

The only thing that is constant, the only thing that never leaves, is this. You can go out of here and go down the road and there will still be this. It doesn't matter what you do or where you go, there'll always be this. You can never escape the lover, the absolute, the no-thing. You can never escape the one, because you already are the one. The one is all there is.

The whole point of what we are talking about here today is giving up any idea that there is anyone anywhere. There isn't anyone, so there is nothing to do, there is nothing that can be done. Look for 'me' – where is 'me'? Nowhere. All there is is this. All there is is the seeing of this. Whatever that is – feeling warm, hearing a sound, sitting on a chair, feeling angry, feeling frustrated – all of these things are simply sensations. There is no fixed datum called 'me' in there – there are just happenings. The one that sees that is what is.

Can one avoid the one?

One is apparently avoiding the one most of the time – although there is nothing to avoid, of course.

So one can also not avoid the one?

Yes, but the same answer applies – there is only one and so avoidance is also oneness.

How does that work?

It's a paradoxical mystery. In a way, we are back to the beginning. The giving up of the searching for oneness is not the avoiding of oneness. But there isn't anyone who can bring that about – it just happens. It isn't that grace happens – it is that all there is is being.

It doesn't matter if you don't understand any of this – in fact, it's better not to understand. Something else knows this; something else is open. At the point when the body dies, and when the mind which maintains the idea of continuation and separation dies, there is only light. There is only the seeing of love – which is all there is. All this is just love appearing in the drama as division. When the drama apparently ceases, all there is is love. But it's a love which is beyond the heart of man, beyond any imagination that we have about love.

Is that what Osho meant when he said 'Never born, never died'?

Yes. A good way of seeing it is to imagine a light in a projector and there is a film put in called 'Tony Parsons'. The film runs through and at the end it drops out; and there is still only the light. It is the light that allows the film to be. There is only light. You could go a bit further and say that it won't be you that sees the light, because there is only light. It isn't you that awakens – it is you that drops away, and there is light. That's another way of trying to explain the unexplainable.

o   o   o

When I was in the fish shop this morning buying fish, there was a very nice feeling that there was only this. It was very soothing in a way.

When there is only this, there is a sort of sweetness about it. We get in the way and want to make this something else. And that is also this. The mind adopts the idea of making this better or making it something else and gets hold of it, and we're back in the race again. That's OK, it's divine. It's only that when there is a seeing of that, there is a stepping out of the apparent prison, and there is a fragrance of freedom, a sweetness, in that.

125

So searching for truth is a bit like making love in an attempt to find virginity – it's actually denying it.

Yes, searching for truth is denying it. Searching for one is a continual denial of the realisation that one is all there is.

o o o

When there is no one, there is clear seeing. Everything is simply seen as it is. All the time there is a seeker, the seeker looks at what he thinks are objects in order to get something from them. So when he looks out, he looks out with arrows. When there is no one, then what seemed to be out there, instead of being out there, floats back into the nothing. In seeking there is a projection out. When there is no seeker, everything is seen as floating in and is accepted just as it is. It is what it is, and it is totally accepted by no one.

In the end, there is no sense of there being an individual who things float into; there is no idea of something being seen. Everything arises in love. Everything is love. When there is no one, there is simply that unicity. There's no question of anything needing to change or anything needing to be better or worse – it just is what it is.

That is what I mean when I use the word 'beloved'. What is seen is seen simply as the beloved arising. That is where oneness is seen by no one. That is the natural being we all long for. And actually that is the being that is already there. We think it isn't. We expect there to be some sort of price, some sort of gift for us in what is out there. All the time we are looking for that, we are not seeing what is already there. Awakening is simply the dropping of looking for something. It's the dropping of the one that seeks. That's all it is.

And once that acceptance is there, there is also an acceptance of the character, the character in the play, the 'me'. There is an acceptance of this body/mind organism that walks around on this stage. It is simply seen and taken in, in love. Once there is an acceptance of this character, then there is an acceptance of all the other apparent characters. It is seen that that is simply all the one manifesting.

This is really what unconditional love is. Unconditional love comes from there being no one. It comes out of nothing. All the time there is someone there, there is an idea about how we should love; there is a technique for loving people and forgiving them and trying to understand them. It is the attempt of the mind trying to reach to some love that is beyond the idea of a technique of love. So awakening is simply clear seeing, seeing of what is.

Somehow what goes on here is a communication with the clear seeing, with the wisdom that is in all of us. When absolute clarity is heard by absolute clarity which is overlaid by confusion, the absolute clarity can take over; confusion can drop away. The idea that anything can be done about dropping the 'me' falls away, and what also falls away with it is the 'me' …

I had a wonderful experience this morning—there was a sudden acceptance of 'me'-ing. There was real acceptance that 'me'-ing and twoness is superimposing itself on the original unity. There was the feeling, 'I have been "me"-ing all my life, so why the hell should I change? It's a habit, just like smoking. Let twoness prevail if it wants to'. That kind of a feeling was there. It was very relaxing.

I think one of the most difficult things about this is the sense of identity. It's easier to see a tree and to let it simply be a tree or be even the lover, tree-ing. But when we see this identity, this thing we think is 'me' … That is the most difficult thing, to allow that to be there without any sense that it should be different.

Is it the longing for pure innocence?

Yes, absolutely. Actually, we walk around in innocence. We are actually like children walking around in the wonder of this. But we've taken on board adulthood, which tries to get something out of this, wants to do a deal with this. And that is OK, it's the divine play. But we are never really happy with that; there is something missing in that; that dealing overlays something else that we know is in everything. We *know* everything is the appearance of the ineffable.

○   ○   ○

Is the ego the same as the mind?

Well, they both tend to be identities. We tend to think of the mind as a thing – really, it is a collection of thoughts. One of the thoughts is 'I am a separate entity', which you could call the formation of an ego. The ego is the idea that there is a separate entity. And there is nothing wrong with that. In a way, freedom is falling in love with this ego, letting that sense of identity just be there. You are living with ego; you are living with other apparent egos – let them be there.

Can you say something about how that works?

When we are babies, basically there is simply oneness, but there is no recognition of that. There is only paradise, but there is not a knowing of being in paradise. At some point, our mother says to us, 'You are Mary' or whoever; and then there is a dropping into a sense of there being someone looking at something else called a mother. That is the first moment of separation.

Fear is rooted in separation. Fear – the most powerful emotion we have – is actually instigated by the sense of separation. Separation is the root of apparent suffering and loss and longing and need.

Oneness is playing the game of two, being separate in order to come back and find and know oneness. That separate one, over the apparent years, goes on reinforcing the idea of 'me'. It tries to create a world that is comfortable and safe and predictable and known. As that world is built, that 'me' becomes more and more contracted. At some point or other – either at death or before death – what happens is that that contracted 'me' suddenly explodes, is completely lost and thrown out into everything. That is when it is seen that everything is 'me'. That is awakening.

I was wondering how the mind works.

Well, the mind is only a tool that is used by one to divide everything into two. The mind is the divider. The mind lives in time and division. Take away time and division and there is no mind. A lot of religions suggest that that is the way to enlightenment, but in oneness the mind can still function.

Thoughts come into the mind/body of Tony Parsons; they are not generated from here. All of existence arises through the generation of thought from oneness. This room is a thought-form. Oneness is creating the thought of room, and room appears. And actually, it is not one continual appearance – it is manifestation being created and destroyed. Room – no room, room – no room, room – no room ... that is what is actually happening here. But for the 'me', there seems to be a room here. When clear seeing is there, what is seen is room and no room. Which is the same as saying that what is seen is nothing and everything.

o o o

Can I ask a personal question?

Oh, this is going to be exciting!

You've talked about falling in love with your own character and then falling in love with the other characters. When you met your wife ... what made you ask her to become your wife? How does a preference come about?

It all arises in the manifestation. In some way or other, the character in the play melds with another character in the play, in a way that is inescapably more powerful or more wonderful than any other particular meeting.

Certain characters don't fit in with other apparent characters, and there is nothing wrong with not liking or not getting along with somebody. When there is clear seeing, then not liking another character is accepted as what arises. But what you are is totally beyond that – it is the one in which not liking a character or a characteristic arises.

There is nothing wrong or right with that – that is what is happening. It is only the mind that thinks that awakening is about totally loving and accepting everyone. It is the mind's idea of what perfection should look like. We are not talking about perfection here. We are talking about clear seeing – a total acceptance of what is, including not liking someone.

Doesn't the character get milder after awakening?

Yes, likes and dislikes and preferences are not necessarily so powerful anymore. It just doesn't matter.

I can see my mind saying, 'Well, how do I accept everything?' It is brilliant at turning everything into a future-oriented possibility. At the same time, sitting with you, I feel as though the chain has been taken off my bicycle, and I am just pedalling away …

What is being communicated here is totally uncompromising.

It is actually scary in a way, in that it really doesn't lend itself to personal investment. I can't even really call it a fear … It is a benediction, really; a relief. It's paradoxical – it includes a lot of opposites. This is not really a question …

It's gorgeous. For those that hear, this is the end of everything.

How to deal with fear?

You don't deal with fear – all dealing falls away here. There is no dealing but there is fear, so fear is what arises. Finish. End.

All the time there's a thought like, 'This is fear, I'm afraid I must do something about it', then the story is there and the CD goes round – 'He doesn't love me' or whatever. But if you let it be, this thing in here – it is in here, isn't it? *(points to solar plexus)* burning, sort of black with bits of green and all that … Just know that there is something in there and simply see it.

o   o   o

I accept that there is no learning and no process, but does having had glimpses or experiences create a kind of environment where you can easily reunite?

Yes. *You* don't, but certainly what begins to happen with people who come to this sort of meeting (and also with people who never ever hear anything like this) is that the light dissipates what is only apparent darkness. The light is the only thing that is here. This is all only light; this is all only light with bits of colour and movement in it. There is no such thing as darkness – darkness is just less light. So the light dissipates the apparent darkness.

Is it possible that the mind gets an idea and labels it as God?

Yes, absolutely. The mind lives in references and pigeon-holes and names and labels. And even whilst this process is going on, it might put a label on and say that enlightenment is happening.

Is it OK that the mind does that?

Absolutely. Everything is OK. The only difficulty is that there can be an identification with the mind's information – then there can be the idea of adopting some sort of process that will make what is already happening happen quicker. But it doesn't matter.

So whether I stay in bed or come here doesn't matter?

Staying in bed would have been perfect – as would coming here.

○   ○   ○

You say that thoughts or emotions come in. Does that mean they come inside?

Everything is really only arising in being. Me sitting here is actually arising in that. As there is only oneness, there isn't an inside and an outside. We tend to think of things as outside and we try to get something from them. The wall isn't over there – it is arising in this. There isn't an 'out there' – there is only being in which everything manifests.

Doesn't thought take place in the brain?

No, it only actually arises in being. For me, the brain is simply a computer; it is something else that arises in being. There is only the appearance of the brain and thought arises in being. Nothing can be except in being.

○   ○   ○

Does it make you lonely to be realised?

At first there is a feeling of being alone, because there is a seeing that what has been seen apparently isn't seen by anyone else. Also there is a sense that there is no way it can be communicated. In another way of course, you are the one that isn't alone – everything is your lover. Everybody else is actually lonely because they can't find their lover.

After Tony Parsons walked across the park, there was quite a strong moving in and out. When there is a moving out, there is a sense of being alone in that. Now there is no longer any sense of anything like that.

What happened in the park was that not only was there the seeing of 'I am all that is', but also there came the seeing 'All there is is this'. Thereafter, there was a great dedication to this by Tony Parsons. In the 'me'-ing there was a great dedication to going back into the being. I still thought there was a choice to be made. The only thing I could do was what I called switching on, which was to bring my awareness back to sitting on a chair or whatever. For a time, I thought I was doing that. For a while, I still thought there was somebody who could choose.

Quite a while after that, the last piece of the jigsaw fell into place.

o   o   o

Can you give us any advice?

Yes – don't take advice! No, really, basically there is nothing. This is one of the few places where you pay money to get nothing.

It sells well!

Yes, but it doesn't sell anywhere near as well as a place where you go to get something. That's much more popular. This is reassuringly unpopular.

o   o   o

Could you say that there are layers of understanding?

Yes, but the final understanding is the realisation that there is nothing to understand.

As far as communication is concerned, there is no question at all that the only clear communication is out of nothing into nothing. This is nothing talking to nothing, and nothing is, if you like, sitting out there and shouting 'Hurrah!' But the mind that is trying to overlay that is shouting 'Oh no!' or 'Yes, but ...' There is only one communication, and that is nothing to nothing. Any idea that there are different levels at which you speak to people is just ignorance or arrogance.

I had a time not so long ago when I had a lot of experiences of oneness. That's gone now. My mind sometimes thinks I am further away than I was before.

I don't use the word 'experience' because it implies that there is an experiencer, but moments of oneness can happen and then apparently not be there anymore for a while. It varies from person to person. But it is all totally regulated – there is only so much oneness that the body can stand, and then it needs to go back into contraction, until the time comes when that can be totally accepted by the body. It's a very energetic thing.

Is it important to follow your longing?

No. There is no way to follow longing – there is just longing.

o   o   o

When Tony became not-Tony, was there any idea of going back and asking somebody for forgiveness, for example? Did anything like that come up?

It didn't come up, simply because it was seen that there is nothing to forgive and no one to forgive.

So no guilt?

No guilt, no. Guilt and the sense of responsibility fell away very quickly – in fact, they virtually vanished overnight. I have a feeling that guilt and a sense of responsibility fall away quite quickly for a lot of people. Who is there to be guilty or responsible … and for what? Nothing is happening.

Amsterdam
December 2002

There's somebody in America – very fussy, very pedantic – who read *As It Is*. He wrote to us with all sorts of criticisms – 'Why have you got illustrations in the book? How can you illustrate this? … Did you know that somebody wrote about the open secret in 2002 BC? Why didn't you acknowledge that at the front of the book? … You say that one moment of presence is worth more than a thousand years of good work. How did you work that out? Is it exactly a thousand years?'

Something in the book really frightened him, I feel. Somewhere he wanted to reject it by focusing in on things that were totally unimportant.

He sent another e-mail a week later saying he'd thrown the book across the room in disgust – but then he'd picked it up again. He said, 'I read the book again and something awful happened – it got up and hit me in the face'.

Somewhere he suddenly saw something that a week before he hadn't wanted to see. He'd suddenly seen what the book was *really* saying, and that completely blew away all the ideas he'd had about what was wrong with it. He used a lovely expression – he wrote, 'What I've done for years and years is to try and understand enlightenment; I've tried to work it all out. And now I see that that is like trying to take the ocean home in a jam-jar'. I also like the expression that Alan Watts used – 'Trying to understand God is like trying to fall in love with a kilometre'.

So what I want to say today is that really it's not about trying to understand – there is no way that this can be understood. What is going on here is sharing something which is totally beyond the mind, which is not of the mind at all. The mind can comprehend the words and the mind can have concepts about the nature of reality or the nature of enlightenment. In that sense, mental communication is taking place here today. But what we are really doing here is putting the mind in its place. Mind is simply a tool that oneness uses – oneness uses the mind to create two.

As we grow up, we listen to the mind and we think that it's going to guide us. We try to work out how to make our lives work, using the mind as our guide. And when it doesn't work out which of course it never does – we think we can use the mind to find something which is beyond the mind.

There is no way the mind can lead us anywhere at all in that sense, because the mind lives in time, and what we are talking about here is not in time at all. What we are talking about here is already this, which is timeless. Awakening is meeting the timeless. Awakening is out of time and out of space. But the mind will listen to what is being said here and make a list and try to turn it into something that can be taken away.

We were having dinner with a friend last night and he said, 'What's wonderful about what you are saying is that it isn't portable. You can't take it away and put it on your desk and open it and say, "Well, this is what Tony's talking about. This is what I've now got to invest in or follow or do"'.

It's impossible to get hold of anything that is going on here, so don't try and make a mental list or try to understand the concepts. It's a dropping of all concepts about becoming anything or about being on a path. Basically, all there is is this – there is just this.

Enlightenment has nothing to do with you. It has nothing to do with personal change. Get the sense of there being no one sitting there. Get the sense that all there is is space, that all you are is space – just space, in which things apparently happen. When that begins to take over, then somehow the self drops away – it's only a mirage anyway – and all that is left is being what is.

To the mind 'what is' is very ordinary, nothing special. When 'what is' is seen in an uncluttered way, when it is simply and clearly seen, it is full of wonder. Just seeing the manifestation arising and then falling away, arising and falling away – that is all that is happening. It is an absolute miracle.

And what arises is meaningless. It's not trying to get anywhere – it's just a flower garden. And it includes everything – pain, suffering, frustration … All those things are simply arising and falling away. When they arise in clear seeing, all the worries and anxieties simply arise and fall away. There is no one to hold on to them – they can't lock into anyone.

But all the thoughts that come in – they belong to *me* – they don't come in for you or for someone else. The thoughts that arise in that body/mind arise uniquely for that body/mind to discover that there is no one there having those thoughts. But yes, the thoughts that arise there are not like the thoughts that arise there *(pointing to someone else)*. His wall is his wall – your wall is your wall.

But it is not that they are personalised in the sense that they have any meaning – they are personalised because they are the lover. All the time there is an apparent person there, what happens is personalised. It is uniquely there for that seeker to discover that there is only oneness. It is love, unconditional love, which knows that that seeker needs this, to discover oneness.

And there is no goal?

No.

So it's sort of crazy?

It's crazy love. Love *is* crazy. Love has no regard for this world.

Love overruns and overturns this world and embraces it. It makes a nonsense of this world. The reality makes a nonsense of the way we think the world is, that it has purpose and is taking us somewhere. There is nowhere to go – there never has been. We live in a sort of madness, doing this and that, trying to do this and that, and what we are looking for is already here. What we look for is in what is, but we think we'll find it over there.

There is only the one, there is only the source, and so everything that arises is the source. Presence isn't something that is over there that you have to find – there is only presence. Right now, there is only presence; all there is is the one. The thoughts that come in are the one thinking … The searching that comes in is the one searching for itself. Everything that is apparently happening is simply oneness manifesting. There is nothing but oneness. So you can't get it wrong.

o   o   o

Yesterday evening I couldn't sleep, and that's rare for me. It was following something you'd said – it felt like a kind of structure was falling apart. It was so empty and so nothing … There was no 'me', and it was so strange, and frightening in a way.

At first it can be a bit frightening because it feels like it's too much freedom. 'I want to go back into a confinement of some sort where I feel I'm still running the show'.

Yes, it feels safer to be in the 'me' – it's something to keep you busy or to worry about.

Oh absolutely. I think it was Ouspensky who said, 'The most difficult thing to drop is your suffering'. The 'me' is something we've grown up with – we're familiar with it, we really believe in it. So when it starts to evaporate, it's like losing an old friend.

Sometimes I feel that what some might call negative arisings, such as fear and anger, are somehow like temptations to come back to the 'me'. It's as if they're saying, 'Come back here'.

It's nice and cosy.

I find it really difficult to say, 'No thanks'.

There's somebody in England who talks about struggle a lot, struggling to find this. To hold on to that struggle is to hold on to an identity. In his case the identity is actually virtually gone, but the one thing that keeps it there is the struggle.

o   o   o

When you can't really believe your own suffering, you also can't really believe the suffering of others, and that irritates people a lot.

Yes, that's threatening. What you're really saying is that the suffering arises but it is not owned by anybody; there is nobody suffering. And that is a threat in the normal world.

It makes it harder to have a normal conversation, or what people call a normal conversation.

And then that also passes, and you can have very normal conversations. I have normal conversations with my father-in-law every time I take him shopping. I pick him up in the morning and we have these wonderful conversations where he says, 'It's all very well for these politicians because they can promise anything to get votes but when it comes down to it they never deliver the goods!' And I play the part and join in and say, 'Yes, you're quite right.'

In a way he is right. Everybody is right … The *mind* is always trying to prove itself right.

o   o   o

On the one hand, there's this longing for awakening – on the other there seems to be more and more resistance. How can you deal with the resistance?

It's the same for everybody, really. Most people have great expectations about discovering what they are and they think awakening is going to be the answer to everything. And yet they're also really frightened of it …

But *you* can't deal with it – although it can be seen that all there is is resistance; all that is arising is resistance. Don't fight it – *you* can't do anything, there is no one there.

What can become clear is that nothing is the enemy. There isn't a thing called 'resistance' which is fighting against oneness resistance is oneness; resistance is the one resisting, oneness resisting its own self-discovery. That's the drama – the resistance to seeing that there is only oneness. That's the game that's created. All that is happening here is oneness resisting its own self-discovery.

Everybody has got it – we *are* it. What's going on here is the exposing of the idea that you *haven't* got it. Everybody has it but they don't know that, and they long for it. And the longing is divine. That's what is wonderful about this – this is absolutely perfect; this is oneness manifesting itself. And whatever form that takes, it is absolutely divinely perfect. It doesn't need to change.

That makes it sound very peaceful.

Not necessarily, no. If we can only be peaceful, we are in another prison called 'being peaceful'. Of course, there *is* a peace in it, there is something wonderful about residing as this …

Life will always juggle around with you and knock you about – until oneness takes over and there is simply that. Then life goes on as it always has, but there isn't anyone to be juggled or knocked.

Do things intensify before change happens?

For some people they do but there are no rules. Certainly all the time there is someone there seeking, something will come and disturb that in exactly whichever way it needs disturbing. There are some people who live in what I call a glass box. They are very detached, but it is somehow a personal detachment. The glass box gets shattered by life – and then there is love.

It's a real challenge to love those arisings that feel difficult.

Well, it's a challenge but it's a challenge that you don't have to take up, because there is no one there to take it up. It's just happening.

o o o

Can you say something about inspiration, as it can arise for artists or composers? I've had myself the experience of how well things go when I'm not there.

For what you might call an artist or composer there can be a clear seeing or a sense of no one being there through the talent. You could say, for example, that Mozart was not there anymore when the music came through him. But it seems that that was true only in the area of music – I believe that he found it quite difficult to deal with the world.

Is music the sound of oneness?

Well, everything is the sound of oneness. Not just Bach and Mozart – roadworks as well … There is no way that oneness expresses through beautiful music or art more than it does through anything else. Garage music is silence making a noise. Emotionally and culturally, you may think that there is a difference, but that is personalised and conditioned experience; it has nothing to do with awakening.

People think that awakening is about being spiritual. I know somebody who says that Turner is nearer to expressing consciousness than Picasso because Picasso's work is all from the ego. It's absolute nonsense, statements like that, making one thing more sacred than another. Otherwise one should only look at Turner paintings and only listen to Mozart – and you're straight into another prison.

So there's no place for effort?

Who is going to make the effort? Find the person who can choose to make the effort. As far as what we are is concerned, it has nothing to do with making an effort. In the world you could say that effort achieves something – and so if effort achieves, then we can achieve enlightenment. Many teachings are based on the idea that they are speaking to someone who has choice and can make an effort to attain something called enlightenment. That is rooted in a deep ignorance.

Does it not help at least to have an interest in attaining enlightenment?

Awakening is not about attaining something – it's about losing something. The interest that you may have in that is not *your* interest – there is nobody there to have an interest – interest arises. But there are people who have no idea what we are talking about here and have no interest in it at all, and awakening can happen.

What interests me is that people seem to understand this more now than a few years ago. What's happening?

These days, this message, if you like, is being delivered totally directly; before it was delivered in an obscure way. It's very apparent that people are open to hearing this directly. Bang! Nothing obscuring it.

o   o   o

What is the source of it all?

All *is* the source. There is only the source. This manifestation is source manifesting. There is only being, and what arises in being is 'me'-ing. You pretend that there is a 'me', and you have pretended to yourself for so long that you actually believe it's true. You've fallen into the belief that there is someone there.

Why?

Why not? It's love overflowing. Love overflows and manifests as one being two. All of this is negative and positive charges appearing as walls and fish and bodies. And the consequence of twoness is the game of paradise lost – we lose paradise in order to find it again. It's a game, it's the drama of one looking for itself.

Out of oneness arises the longing to come home, and also the fascination of not coming home. It is in a sort of dream called 'me living a life that is fascinating', where there is a drive to make that life work. Because when you've made a lot of money and have a good wife and good health and all the usual things, then you've created something you could call home, a kind of artificial home. But it never is really satisfying, because always there is the longing to be at one.

That is the drama, and that drama is going absolutely nowhere. It is just there for the player to discover he is everything, including the stage, the audience, the lights ... All that is happening is meaningless, but it is so beguiling and fascinating that the mind is absolutely sure it has meaning and that it will lead somewhere. It never gets there, but it always seems to be leading somewhere.

o   o   o

Tony, I like some things in the world so much – art, music ... I also feel a very strong attachment to people, and I have the feeling that this attachment is in the way.

Yes, it can be.

I think it's painful to be so attached to people, circumstances, places ...

143

The pain is inviting you to see that what you are is beyond attachment. Everything that is happening in the drama is telling you that there is something else.

I feel I can't let go of that attachment.

No, you can't. But in some way or other, directly there is a hearing that there is something else and that there is no one there, that there is actually no attachment, only the appearance of attachment – directly that is heard, something else starts to happen.

Attachment falls away?

In the end 'you' fall away – what falls away is 'you', and with that everything. It is you that has the attachment – you are the rich woman. You can have no money at all but still be full of attachment.

If I get enlightened, I feel that I will lose my family, things will have no meaning for me anymore, and I'm afraid of that.

Yes of course, who wouldn't be? You are going to lose everything – what you think is everything. All the time there is a 'me' there, it has a collection of things around it that keep it as 'me'. And those things are everything to that 'me'. That's why Christ said, 'It is more difficult for a rich man to enter the kingdom of heaven …' Or, 'What does it profit a man if he gains the whole world …?' And by 'world' he meant things like family, children, music – all the things that maintain the sense of a 'me'.

When the 'me' falls away, all of those things go; you lose everything. And in the letting go of that – which *you* can't do – there is nothing left but everything. When there is nothing, there is everything. And then music and children take their place in that, let's say, rather than being the things that maintain the 'you'. For the first time – and that is what is so beautiful and wondrous about this – there is a real love for the children and the music rather than the attachment which maintains the 'you'.

144

Somebody in London the other day said, 'Suppose I told you I was an addict ...' I said, 'Well, everybody in the room is an addict, actually'. Not necessarily an addict to drugs or gambling or alcohol but mainly to 'me' – we are all addicted to the drug of 'me' and all that comes with it. When that falls away and there is no longer any addiction, there is just life. You aren't anyone – you are life. Once there is no one, there is just the seeing of life. There is just liberation living.

The falling away of the 'me' seems to take time.

It seems to the apparent seeker that it takes time. It isn't actually like that, because there is no 'me' – there is only being, and it is timeless.

Sometimes there seems to be a great clarity and sometimes it seems to be foggy, dusty ...

There comes a time when it is just there.

There comes a time, you say ...

Well, as far as the mind is concerned. Michael Reid would tell you that there came a time when there was simply being. He is only giving you information. In fact, he knows and I know that there never was a time when there was anything other than just being.

For me, I feel the addictive part is getting stronger.

That does happen. Often, when people get near to this, it seems that the lure of what they most value gets stronger, as if to try and hold them in the dream. Not for everyone is it like that, but it is for some. For others, it simply evaporates.

o   o   o

Listening to this, one is struck by the simplicity of it, and yet the mind wants complexity.

Yes, the mind hates it – it sits here and wants to do something with it. When somebody comes from nothing and says nothing which is really what is going on here – then what other people do is get hold of that, take it into their minds and re-interpret it.

It's fascinating how it becomes so complicated. There are probably five hundred different schools of Buddhism, six hundred different Christianities ... The actual reality is totally simple and direct – this is it. But as soon as the mind gets hold of that – or tries to get hold of that – it has to complicate it. It has to divide it into the many.

This game of hide and seek which we're playing – is it moving in any direction?

No, there is no direction. There never has been a direction. There is nothing going anywhere. There is no destiny because there isn't anywhere to go. It is only in the mind that we think that there is what is called God's will, or that everything is moving towards something. Nothing moves – nothing has ever moved.

I've never come across any clear and absolutely non-dualistic teachings up until this time. There were teachers like Christ, Buddha, Lao Tzu who did teach the direct path, but it has since been obscured. Now it is totally naked and open. You could say, if you think in terms of the story of the world, that now the teaching has become very direct and uncompromising and it is available not in many places, but it is around.

But actually all you're talking about is appearance. Nothing happens – nothing has ever happened. The appearance is unconditional love appearing, and in order to appear as the invitation, it appears with a total balance on both sides. What the mind thinks of as good in the world is equally balanced by what the mind thinks of as bad. There is in fact no such thing, but that is the appearance. It has to appear in total neutrality so that there can be a recognition that the whole of the appearance is without purpose or direction.

It's beautiful, it's absolutely exquisite. It is unconditional love saying, 'Look, here is a world that appears to be going somewhere and there are all kinds of battles going on, but actually it isn't going anywhere at all'. I can't make my life work and we are never going to save the world, because it is in total balance all the time.

What is it really saying? It is saying that there is only oneness. That's the whole beauty of it. Its pointlessness is its beauty.

All I can say is, 'There is only this'. This is silence making a noise; this is stillness moving. But there is no way to explain it there is no way the mind can ever accept this or comprehend it.

o   o   o

I have the idea that I should learn something, that I should take home with me what I hear here.

You try to remember it, do you?

Yes.

Don't. What is happening here is something that is far deeper and more dramatic than the words. What is happening is that the 'me' is just falling away. The more this is heard, the more the 'me' falls away. There is nothing the 'me' can do about the falling away – it just falls away. You don't need to know that – you don't need to remember anything that is being said here. 'You' are being taken over … It's too late now. Something is being heard inside, which can never be forgotten. The mind can try to devalue it but it will always be remembered and finally recognised.

Why should I come here?

There is nothing you can do about coming here or not coming here. Just as there is nothing you can do about hearing or not hearing what is going on here. Isn't that wonderful? Don't worry – all that is really going on is totally beyond 'you'.

Is there a kind of battle?

There *appears* to be a battle between 'me'-ing and being ... Although being isn't actually in the battle – it's the 'me' that fights.

I have the feeling that many people are afraid of giving up the 'me' and just saying 'yes' to whatever is arising.

I'm not saying that. I'm not talking about acceptance or saying yes or no. In a way, talking about acceptance and surrender and saying yes is another sort of teaching. Directly the mind hears that it is a good idea to accept everything, it goes and accepts everything – for three or four hours maybe. It's the same with saying 'Be here now' ... It's just nonsense, just the mind getting hold of some idea – 'Say yes' ... 'Surrender' ... Who is going to surrender? Who wants to anyway?

What can you do then?

Nothing. *It* is being done. This is it. There is no one there to do anything. Whatever is happening is it. There is nothing which isn't the one. If you can't see it, that is the one not seeing it.

And that is the joke. When awakening happens, people laugh and laugh. The thing they've been trying to get hold of, all the searching they've done only to discover that already there is only that – it's an amazing joke.

All the time there is someone seeking, there is someone looking for something to happen. After it has apparently happened, then it is seen that nothing happened. People say to me, 'What you are doing or what you are communicating is about destroying the seeker'. But there is no one who can destroy the seeker. All the time there is a 'me', seeking will happen. It's got to happen, because that is the whole drive of 'me', to find that which it is longing for. Nothing can stop that until the 'me' is no more, until the one that is looking around for it suddenly sees that everything *is* it.

○   ○   ○

To whom are you talking?

I am not talking most of the time. Tony Parsons comes into this, but actually it is coming through ... from nowhere. No one is talking to no one. This isn't one mind talking to another – it is nothing talking to nothing. Obviously it uses words, because there is a mind there. There is a communication on that level as well, but basically what is going on is nothing communicating to nothing. There is something going on in this room that is underneath the words.

The difficulty is that the words that come out of nothing are caught by the mind. The mind is like a dream-catcher. It catches the words and turns them into something it can use to present the idea that there is somewhere to go and something to get. It is continually filtering out reality and turning it into an unreality.

Basically, that is what we do. After childhood, the mind turns everything into an unreality. The unreality is that you live in a world of separation. That is intentional, that's divine, but we take it seriously. We are on a stage, in a play or a parable called 'Life', but we believe it is real and we believe that it matters.

Would you say what is going on here is the slow erosion of the mind and the producing of mind-exhaustion?

Yes, though it's not always slow. Somebody in London might come to a few meetings and the mind just gives up. Of course, it can happen in an instant. The mind gives up and takes its natural place. Its natural place is just to be a tool, instead of what it has been, sitting on the throne apparently running it all.

149

It gives up any effort to understand?

Yes. The whole thing about the effort to understand is that it keeps you on a path. In a way, obviously you have to come to some sort of understanding that there is nothing to understand. But when you reach there, where do you go? You've lost everything, you see.

One of our great possessions is our understanding. If you come here enough times – or even once – you can lose that totally and suddenly you are confronted with *this*. And it is just wonderful.

Understanding and seeking are one thing?

Yes, they are.

But a wonderful arising is also meaningless.

Absolutely. Everything is meaningless ... It is still wonderful! To no one. That is its beauty, that it is meaningless. It's not going anywhere – it's just oneness, this is it. It isn't selling anything to anyone – it's just what it is. That is total freedom. That is the only revolution.

What is the essential difference between before you walked in that park and after?

The only essential difference is that before I walked in the park there was somebody who was seeking; there was a 'me'. All the time there is a separate 'me', there is a disquiet which causes or creates seeking. The whole divineness of 'me' is that it creates the seeker, the search to discover that there is no 'me'. And when there is no 'me', there is simply this, oneness. And that is the constant.

Are you always then not aware of self?

There is no one here to be aware of self or aware of oneness. There is no one here. In fact, there is no one there, there is no one in this room – there is just oneness. But in that oneness the self can appear.

So your mind never thinks back to the point where there was a Tony Parsons?

No, it can't. In fact, neither can you. You can't even think back to last night. You can tell me now what happened last night, but that is what is happening right now. Last night doesn't exist – it never did.

So you can never be accurate?

No, you can't. What you are saying about last night is what you are saying right now. It isn't last night. Last night there was *this*.

And if you tell me what happened last night now, there is *this*.

○   ○   ○

Are there people who don't seek?

No, there is no such thing as a non-seeker. All the time there is an identity, there is a sense of loss. In very simple terms, when we are kids, when we are tiny, we are pure being, but we don't know we are. Then one day, our mother walks through the door and says, 'You are John'. And suddenly you become John and she becomes your mother. That is the moment of separation.

Directly there is separation, seeking starts. When separation begins, you are out of paradise. You have apparently lost paradise and immediately you seek it.

What you see in a baby is what you are. The difference is that when that is as it were re-discovered, then there will be a knowing of that, whereas with the baby there is just that, without any sense of knowing it.

That is the whole point of this. We go out of paradise in order to come back to it and know it. We can't know it if we haven't lost it.

The whole game of self-identity is a fascinating game. We bang our head against the wall and we think in some way or other that we can make that pleasurable. Seeking is banging your head against the wall – finding is stopping banging your head against the wall. There is nothing to find.

Why do we do it?

We don't do it – it happens. We think there is nothing else in the world but self-identity. We think we have a life and we are absolutely sure – or the mind is absolutely sure – that we can make that life work. That is the fascination – 'I'm going to make my life work, by one means or another ...'

When it is finally realised that we never will, that is the whole gift. Disappointment is the whole gift of life, from the beloved. When we realise that, then the last resort is to become enlightened. But the mind also gets hold of that and says, 'Oh well, this is the last thing that is going to make it finally work. This is an object that I can get hold of to make my life work'. It's the final mind-game. And still we are banging our head against the wall.

Sitting here, there is so much frustration coming up about doing and seeking and wanting so much to get somewhere ...

It's hugely powerful. It drives you on and on.

I feel I can't go on anymore. (The questioner is crying.)

But you can't stop going on ... What is the feeling in the body?

It feels hot and restless.

So all there is is that. I know there is a whole thing about the search and the frustration, but actually, in very simple terms, all there is is the heat, the motion. That is all that can be seen – that is all you need to see. That is the gift – just seeing that.

If I were to say to you, 'Go into your past and describe the search and what you're looking for, your life story', we would be here for three hours and get absolutely nowhere, because all we'd be doing is reinforcing the idea that there is someone there who can get somewhere. Forget the story, forget the frustration and the searching – which actually isn't there right now. What is there right now is heat. So see heat.

But you call it a gift.

Well, it is a gift. Whatever arises is the gift – sitting on a chair, drinking water, holding somebody's hand, hearing the car go by, feeling the heat in the body ... It's the gift. This is the bridegroom inviting marriage. And it is always totally simple. It's a feeling, an emotion ... it's a touching, a hearing ... arising and being seen.

Do away with any idea of going into the story; it's the mind that wants to delve into the story. In fact, it is really beautiful; it's absolutely simple. This is it.

There is always one thing. If you really stop, there is only one thing – rubbing your brow, having a sip of tea, a feeling of anger ... I'm talking about something absolutely immediate and direct.

There is always something that is not involved, you said.

In a way, you could say that it is not involved in that it doesn't have any investment. It is the energy from which everything arises. It is the one constant – it is the only constant. It is the unchanging constant silence of what we are. Everything arises out of that.

Let's be clear about this – it is a mystery. You are never going to work this out. In a way, words are completely useless. All the words that are used here are lies. If there is a readiness to hear something else that is happening under the words, then there is a readiness to hear it. If there isn't, then it won't be heard. It's as simple as that. Mind will do anything not to hear this. Anything at all.

o   o   o

A professor of mathematics sent a fax to his wife. It read, 'Dear wife, You must realise that you're 54 years old now, and I have certain needs which you just can't satisfy anymore. Otherwise, I'm happy with you as a wife, so I sincerely hope you won't be hurt or offended to learn that by the time you receive this letter, I'll be at the Grand Hotel with my 18-year-old teaching assistant. I'll be home before midnight'.

When he arrived at the hotel, there was a fax waiting for him. It read, 'Dear husband, You're 54 years old yourself, and by the time you receive this, I'll be at the Breakwater Hotel with the 18year-old pool boy. Being the brilliant mathematician that you are, I'm sure you can easily appreciate the fact that 18 goes into 54 a lot more times than 54 goes into 18. Don't wait up'.

Berlin
January 2002

There is only source appearing ...

In the film projector, there is light, a constant light. And the film – which is your life, the film of Tony Parsons or whatever – runs through the projector. It runs through with all the characters on it and at the end it falls out and isn't there anymore.

What you are is the light, eternal light. The light is the nothing from which everything arises. And what also arises is this character sitting here. You are the presence, the absolute, the nothing, or the light which allows that character to be there.

Is the light creating the story?

There is no creation and no story – only the appearance. You see, this is difficult, because in a way the story emanates from the light, but the light is timeless, totally impersonal and still. Therefore there isn't something in the light making the story up. The story just manifests. It's not something that can be understood ... It is the divine mystery.

And what is even more difficult to understand is that there isn't a purpose or a journey – there is only this. There never was a beginning and there never will be an end. There never was a moment where, let's say, the source rested and didn't know itself and then wanted to know itself and created this. That never happened – nothing ever happens. There is only the eternal this.

There apparently is a story – here is Tony Parsons and there is the world – but it's just an image. And it is only one image – there is only one image. The mind makes it into a series of images called a story. But actually, it is always only one image. It is light … It is oneness.

This is beyond understanding. It is a mystery – the mind can never conceive of this.

There isn't something which is at rest and which then creates something. In the eternal manifestation is the rest, the stillness and the movement, the emptiness and the fullness – everything. And until that is seen, there is always that subtle separation of 'me seeing consciousness manifesting'.

Words are difficult. There are several words you could use for what I call the source – the light, presence, the absolute, the nothing which is everything, the emptiness, consciousness, the beloved … I often call it the beloved. Those words all mean the one thing.

When I say to you that you are the source, that is strictly speaking not accurate. There is only the source. There isn't anyone there that is the source – there is only the source, there is only presence. There is only being (being is, for me, another word for source) … These are words. They can't express what you are. It's impossible.

Out of the source emanates unconditional love. Stillness is the nature of the source and everything in the world or in the appearance has that nature of unconditional love, stillness, impersonality.

Again, these are words – there is no way in which they really express what is. So you'll have to forgive me for the words. Also really, I should use the word 'apparent' in front of everything I talk about – the apparent 'you', the apparent wall, etcetera … It is all only apparent. It is all only a metaphor, a parable, a suggestion, a reflection of another possibility.

Awakening brings a totally different perception. It is not you who has that perception – it is no one who has that perception. Awakening is the realisation that there is no one there. And when there is no one, all that has been talked about is seen by no one, including the character Bill or Mary; they arise in that.

And all the time there is just one image?

There is only the one image or there isn't. There is only the beloved. There is only the absolute appearing as the particular or not.

Always?

It is eternal. It is not 'always' – it is even more than always. It is all there is. Wherever you go in the world, whatever you see is the source appearing. All you see is the beloved, apparently moving, apparently in something called time. It embraces all those things that seem to make it into a story.

Apparently speeding down the highway there is nothing happening?

There is only an appearance of speeding down something called a highway.

Is there an evolution?

No, that is another part of the dream. That is part of the hypnosis, the idea that we are progressing. Evolution is only an appearance suggesting something else.

And energy stream?

There is energy. There is everything – emptiness and energy, anything you like … And it is all the beloved. Including the illusion of there being a separate person, including the illusion that you don't get it.

If everyone wakes up to this, what then?

Never forget you are talking about an eternal drama. Always this drama includes what you would call unawakened people. (As far as I'm concerned, there's no such thing – I don't see anybody awakened or unawakened.) The drama won't ever stop because it is the drama of the one, the singular becoming the plural. Part of that game, that joy, that *leela*, is the separation. 'I will become two so that I can seek what I am. In becoming two, I will feel separate from what I am'. That is the fun. 'I will feel separate from what I am in order to rediscover what I am'.

This will never end, you know – Afghanistan, the Berlin wall, the Roman Empire ... This will always be the drama – just different names.

What we are really talking about here is something totally simple. It is what is in this room right now. It's what you are. It is all there is.

If you close your eyes, you can feel there is an energy there which you could interpret into the words 'I exist'. Don't name it don't say, 'Oh, this is an energy in the body!' There is simply an energy, 'I exist'. Change that into 'presence' and that is what you are – stillness, the energy of presence ... It is utterly impersonal and still, and it sees what arises. It is very simple and very immediate, and it has walked around with you all your life and watched you doing this and doing that, looking for this and looking for that ... And in the very looking is this presence, that which already is.

There is a sense of existence and then it turns back into 'I exist'. It seems to be very strongly in-built, this sense of ownership.

Certainly. At first people go in and out of this. There is such a strong conditioning about the existence of a 'me' that it is very difficult to let that expand. There is still a need to bring it into the mind/body, to bring it into ownership. But as the presence expands and overtakes and becomes everything, the 'me' that wants to bring it back into contraction just drops away.

We are so contracted into 'me'. For years we work on 'me', making 'me' successful. Awakening is like an explosion of that contracted energy. Suddenly, the little 'me' blows up into everything and there is no 'me' left. 'Me' is everywhere.

The mind is the avoiding?

Yes. And it is brilliantly clever, in that it will tell you that it will take you to enlightenment. It will say, 'We will listen to all this and make a list, and I will then take you to the place of enlightenment ... I will find the object of enlightenment for you. You can have that attainment'. That is in a way the most difficult thing to deal with. The mind always wants some sort of technique, and techniques are the way to avoid. The mind is always cleverly introducing you to ideas which avoid what you are, and they are always complicated ideas invested in time, in becoming.

o   o   o

Until about a year ago, I was running sessions called 'Light Body' seminars, and I loved doing it. But after I went to my first retreat with you, I didn't feel able to do it anymore. I felt I was misleading people, advising them to use certain methods. I felt I was betraying them, because what I was telling them isn't really true. I thought, 'I'm just building up a big spiritual ego'. But now there is a sort of longing to start doing it again, and yet there is another part of me which says, 'You just can't do that'.

What is the part of you that says you can't do that?

The part that says, 'Isn't it all a mind thing, the mind creating this feeling of unity, harmony, truth?'

First of all, there is no such thing as truth, really. It's part of the appearance. The appearance is that there is something called true and something called untrue. There is no truth and there is no untruth. There is only this.

But also, what you are suggesting is that everybody should give up what they are doing when what they are doing is apparently misleading other people. But that's just not possible.

159

That mind/body is in the drama of existence; the expression of that mind/body in the drama is those seminars. There is nothing that can stop that and nothing that can make it go on – it simply happens through that mind/body. There is no one there who could choose to go on or to stop.

The other thing is that all the time you're apparently misleading people, you are offering them their perfect invitation. Being apparently misled is the perfect invitation for them. There are many teachers who apparently mislead, many … You want a list? And that is the divine expression; that is absolutely sacred. There is no one, but all the time there seems to be a separate being out there who comes to you to be apparently misled, that is the perfect invitation for that apparent separate being.

There is no responsibility anywhere – there never has been any responsibility because there is no one. Hitler was not responsible – Hitler was the one appearing as Hitler.

How come I don't feel good not doing it and I also don't feel good doing it?

It is the mind that doesn't feel good. Both of them are your invitation. Open yourself to the seeing that neither matters. Nothing matters because nothing is happening. Nothing is going anywhere. The mind will say, 'Well, in six months' time, I will have done ten more seminars and misled 300 more people'. It's divine, and it's meaningless. Really, all there is is sitting on the seat; all there is is what is arising now. In a week's time, all there will be is sitting on a seat; all there will be is what is arising.

o   o   o

On the one hand it's hopeless – on the other hand it's total fun.

Oh yes! What is wonderful about it is the total freedom of it, and what is frightening about it is that freedom, in a way.

160

It's so disillusioning.

Oh yes, everything falls apart. The ways in which we've made this 'me' more and more powerful are through hope and effort and failure and hope again, and the great illusion of there being a reward. 'If I work hard, then something will come back. It must be like that because my mother told me that'.

Look at people in the world – like filmstars or footballers – who make a real effort and apparently succeed. The footballer trains and trains and gets a huge amount of money and a big car and people clap and shout … It seems like he's got something. But what he is doing is trying to fill a shopping basket which has a hole in the bottom. There is never enough.

Everybody in a way is trying to fill that shopping basket, even in a negative way. The victim wants to fill it with attention – 'Love me – I'm a victim'. But there is never enough because there is always the seeker. There is always the one who thinks that something else is needed. All the money in the world and all the fame is never enough, because always there is the seeker, longing for that which is beyond his grasp. Everyone in the world is a seeker, and seeking is bolstered by the illusion that there is a reward.

Of course, the other thing is that whatever we aim for in the world, there is always some sort of dependence on an object; we are always chasing after an object. Somewhere we know it will never fulfil us, because we know that the final fulfilment is totally without dependence.

For religious seekers, the reward is often heaven after death. That is misleading, because all the time there is this belief that if I become pure, when I die, I'll go to heaven.

But *this* is heaven – this is the kingdom of heaven. You walk in heaven. You can never ever not be walking in heaven. You are walking in the absolute all the time. There is always this – eternally there is only this – and this is the paradise.

If there is no illusion, then there is no fear?

Fear can arise. Anything can arise in this because this is the appearance. But what is different is that there is no one who is afraid. Awakening is the realisation that there is no one and nothing that needs awakening. Therefore there is no one to be awakened and there is no one who *has* anything.

What we are talking about here is total liberation, is total poverty, utter poverty. It's the same as humility. Humility isn't 'I am less than you'. Real humility is 'There is no one'. Poverty is that nothing is owned, including fear, suffering, anger … Nothing is owned but fear can arise.

You see this *(pointing to himself)* isn't an island – this is in the appearance. We are all the appearance and in that appearance fear, jealousy, anything arises. I am that; that arises in this. So if somebody says, 'I am an enlightened person – I have no fear, no pride, no ego, what they're actually saying is, 'I'm separate from you. You have fear but I don't, because I possess enlightenment'.

So after awakening it isn't that one's life is suddenly wonderful and there are no problems. The apparent life of that character continues just as it always did, with the same sort of apparent difficulties. But there is no one there anymore. There never was anyone there. Before awakening, there is an idea that there is someone there who has problems, who suffers, who owns pain. Afterwards there is no one.

I can resonate with what you say, but there is so much suffering … And people do suffer – they really do. I can't accept it.

Who is it that cannot accept? The only way that this can be accepted is by coming to see that there is no one suffering here.

When it is seen *(by no one)* that there is no one suffering here, then it is also seen that there is no one suffering there. And in seeing that there is no one suffering there, there is freedom, there is unconditional love.

But I think the source should know that people are suffering.

The source is the suffering. The source is the appearance. There isn't a source that creates suffering. Suffering is the source apparently suffering. All suffering comes from separation. The game, the play, the drama is to suffer separation and to discover liberation.

o o o

Can madmen also be enlightened?

Absolutely. I would sense that there are people in mental homes who are liberated. I think the world would see the awakened state as a form of madness. And it is – in the view of the world it's madness.

I find I worry a lot about how I act or respond in certain situations. I'm always trying to work out the best way to respond, to such an extent that my mind seems to lock and just won't function at all.

Only because there is no best way to respond – except in the mind. The character that you are will respond in whatever way that character will respond. As Suzanne Segal says, 'Follow the obvious'. For you, there is an obvious way to be or to respond which wouldn't be at all the same for me, necessarily.

But also, go beyond that and see that however you respond, it doesn't matter. It matters to the mind that the right path is taken, but ultimately it doesn't matter at all. If there is the beginning of an opening to the realisation that it doesn't matter, then there is more of a letting go. There isn't that 'I've got to get it right!' You never got it wrong – never in your whole life. Everything that has happened in your life – from what you think of as a major event or a major choice down to every last little nuance – has been absolutely perfect.

o   o   o

What is happening here feels like a support. I don't feel like this when I'm at home.

But you will! The whole of this message is to try and get across that it is always here. At home, or on the tram, or wherever – it doesn't matter where you are, you are always in this.

There is no doubt, though, that in this situation there is an opening, there is a sense of opening. Concepts are falling away in this situation and one is seeing from a different point of view. But there is no need to be here. In a way there is no need for you to come here ever again. Your head is now in the tiger's mouth. It is too late – you are already lost.

When I read books of other teachers, I understand that I have a choice and that I can only be liberated in this incarnation when I have a total commitment to liberation. But it appears that I am not able to give this total commitment.

These ideas are rooted in total ignorance. The whole idea that you should be a certain way – totally committed or utterly honest or very serious – is just nonsense. Who is going to be serious? There is nobody in the whole of existence who has ever achieved that totality, simply because it is based on a misunderstanding. The misunderstanding is that there is someone there who can choose to be, let's say, totally dedicated. I suspect that what has happened is that people have meditated for twenty years on top of a mountain and eaten seeds and got so pissed off that they have given up.

No one can do it – there *is* no one. The whole idea that there is someone there who can do it reinforces the veil. The more powerful the·ego that is going to *do* it, the further away is that which is going to happen.

o   o   o

I don't want to pay compliments but I would just like to tell you that I always had an aversion to gurus. Once when I was on holiday I went to one. He sat there looking at everyone, making 'deep' eye contact ... I feel comfortable with you because you are so simple, so ordinary. It's such a relief. And it is something I always knew, that it's simple.

Thank you.

I felt the same at the beginning of the session, when I didn't have to close my eyes and sing 'OM' or 'get into the energy'.

No, there is nothing to get into. It already is. It's not special. There is nothing that is special. During the retreats in England and in Holland there is a good deal of silence but it comes out of naturalness rather than imposition.

We have an idea that to make an effort is not *it*, or to feel separate is not *it*. In the end, the liberation is that *everything* is it. If there is a feeling of effort, then that's the source appearing as effort. The mind wants to make *it* a special place. 'When this happens, I will be in my source ...' You have to do something, or be worthy or still or pure and then ... Bullshit!

I have the feeling I have to stop doing something.

In a way, yes. Stop the idea that there is anything to do or that there is anywhere to go. This is it. This is it! There is a wonderful resting in that – 'Ah! So we are here already!' And we are always here already ... Even if the thought comes up, 'This isn't it', then that's it. It is all just arising and you are the one that sees that.

All this is is a reminder of what you are. Somehow you've forgotten. You've put it on a shelf called 'innocence' or 'childhood',

165

and taken up from the shelf something called 'adulthood' or 'being separate'. You know this, and somehow here you are remembering.

It is really uncanny to talk to people for whom awakening has happened. They say, 'It's so obvious! So immediate and so natural ...' In a way it's no big deal. In another way it is magnificent. It is what is here now, totally naturally here, uncluttered.

o   o   o

I read the book by Suzanne Segal. What was amazing for me is that she didn't know what was going on with her for such a long time. How was that for you?

When this happened and there was the seeing 'I am that', then actually for me it was totally natural. For some people it is connected with deep suffering or loss – for me, it was from one joy into a greater joy.

When I was a kid (and don't forget, this was during the war), I was quite sure that the only thing worth doing was to find God. I grew up in a Christian background and to my mind, the only thing worth doing was to find God. Why do anything else?

I was absolutely sure that God was everywhere, and that everything held a secret. Everything I was looking at held something which was God telling me the secret. The funny thing was that I always knew I would find the secret. So when I walked across the park, then somehow that was 'Oh! ...Yes ... right ...' It was amazing, this incredible stillness ... But also there was a recognition – 'Oh yes! This is how we naturally are. We overlay that with some idea of a "me", someone being there wanting something'.

There was no fear of going crazy. When it happened, what also came with that was a lot of clarity, seeing. One thing that was seen was that we are always in this invitation.

What I also saw was not that we are forgiven our sins, but

166

that we have never sinned. That was staggering for me at the time, because I'd been quite involved in the church before that. I thought the word 'repent' meant to be sorry for your sins and to vow never to sin again. I read in a book by Nicoll (who was a disciple of Gurdjieff) that 'repent' actually means to turn around and see everything in a new way.

Suddenly I saw that awakening has nothing to do with being worthy. It has nothing to do with 'me'. It has to do with seeing something – it is another way of seeing. It is *the* way of seeing.

Why did Suzanne Segal die so soon afterwards?

The thing with this is that there aren't any reference points. For some people it will be like this – for others it will be like that.

There's a joke about a man who goes to heaven, and when he gets to the gates, Peter says, 'We have to ask you if you were faithful to your wife. If you were totally faithful, we'll give you a car that you can drive around in in heaven'. The man says, 'I have been totally and utterly faithful'. Peter says, 'Yes, our records show that that's actually the case. So here's your car'. And the man is presented with a great big Mercedes.

A little while later, a friend of his arrives at the gates and Peter asks him the same question. He replies, 'I was faithful, except for just the one occasion at a Christmas party … Well, you know how it is …' Peter tells him, 'OK, that agrees with what's in our records. This is the car we're giving you to drive around heaven in'. And he shows him a Renault.

So the man is driving around in his Renault when he comes upon this great Mercedes with his friend leaning on the bonnet and crying his eyes out. He says to him, 'What are you crying about? You've got this beautiful car!'

'Yes,' he replies, 'but I've just seen my wife going by on a bicycle!'

○   ○   ○

What is communicated here is that nobody can become enlightened. There is no such thing as an object called enlightenment, and no person has ever become enlightened. There *is* no singular separate person sitting here. There is no one!

Awakening is simply the dropping away of the seeker, the seeker who looks for something out there and goes on looking. It is the dropping away of the one who wants something. When that drops away, there is what is already always there – simply light, the absolute, the source appearing as this … It is not attained or owned by anyone or anything. It simply is that which is the only constant.

All of this is just the source appearing. It's the one appearing as two … The one playing the game of being the wall … And you are playing the game of believing that you are a person – the only problem is that you take that game seriously.

What is happening here (and elsewhere) is that we are remembering, 'Oh yes, this is a game!' It is only remembering something that you know. As children you knew. Then you took on the mantle of separation, of adulthood, and thereafter bereavement. What happens in the world, what happens with your life, however successful it seems to be, it is never ever enough. Always you long to come home.

What goes on here is that you are given absolutely nothing. Somebody came up to me just before we started and said, 'I really enjoyed yesterday but I've totally forgotten everything that went on'. That's wonderful! Already there is a knowing. What is being communicated here is being communicated to the one who knows everything, who sees everything. It is not a communication to the mind. The mind walks in here with all sorts of concepts about what this is and what enlightenment is. And those concepts can be destroyed, so that, again, one is left with nothing.

What can happen here is that confusion can fall away, the confusion of 'I am this person and I have to become still. I have to still the mind – I have to drop the ego ...' Why drop the ego? The ego is fine. The ego appears in this manifestation. The ego is the source, ego-ing. All those ideas like, 'I should be beyond desire – I should be honest – I should be detached, unidentified ...' – those ideas are mind nonsense.

What we are talking about here is falling in love. When we were kids we were in love with this ... with sandcastles ... So we're going to play with sandcastles again. And the sandcastles are here – we are sitting on them, we drink them and eat them. Everything that we touch and everything that our senses know is the game, the *leela*, presence playing.

How can we change the game? Instead of playing the anger game play the joy game?

We can't. You can't. There is absolutely nothing that you can do. Not only is there nothing that you can do, it is far more than that – it is that there is no one. There is no one there. It's about dropping that sense of 'I am a person who is sitting here and will move into joy instead of anger'. You can't open to the idea that there is no one here, because who is going to open to it?

Somewhere this is being heard, somewhere in there this is already known, there is something saying 'Yes!' There is nothing you can do and there is nothing that needs doing because just as you are, sitting there, is the divine expression.

And it is just totally ordinary. The wall I see is the wall you see. I have to pay income tax as well. When awakening happens, problems don't all fall away, you don't walk around in a wonderful serene sort of glow. It is just the dropping of the idea that there is anything to do or any way to be.

How you are is it. How you are is what is arising. You are it. The way you are, your character, is it. It is beautiful just as it is. Exactly as it is. Those neurotic bits and pieces that you think are not quite right are the source being neurotic. It is divine, absolutely divine. Everything you do is an expression of the divine.

There is nothing you can do about knowing that – the only way it is known is when there is no one who knows it. Awakening is that there is no one. What arises is seen by no one. There is nothing that anyone can do about being no one.

Somebody said yesterday, 'This is an easy option'. What they were saying is that suicide is easy. That is what I am suggesting not that the body dies, but the seeking dies.

That is the main suggestion?

Yes, the suggestion is that the seeker dies. And the other part of the suggestion is, 'How can there be anything to seek when what is happening here is it?' There is nothing to find because this is it.

At the same time, everything in us wants to do something, desires something ...

The liberation we seek is the dropping away of the one that is looking for something over there. When it becomes apparent that this is it, then that effort to find the treasure is no longer there. After that, desires can still be there – like the desire to eat spaghetti rather than watercress ... That can still be there, but there is no longer anyone who invests in that. It is a game. It is a wonderful drama. And nothing matters.

What about our ambitions, our goals? We may be enlightened one day but ...

None of you will be. There is only the light. You are all awakened. All of you are awake, believing that you aren't.

After awakening ambitions can still arise, goals can still arise. Before awakening, the whole idea of a goal is that somehow it will finally fulfil you. Afterwards, it is known that it won't. Then that goal is just another part of the play – there is a joy in running faster or further, or in painting a better painting … There is a joy in it because there is no neurotic drive to fill a sense of loss. It is spontaneous unconditional love, spontaneously acting.

o o o

To me it seems easier to be aware that there is only this when I close my eyes and go inside. As soon as I get engaged with things on the outside, I feel I get caught.

Maybe the invitation for that mind/body is to have the eyes closed quite a lot, while for another mind/body it might be going to the pub and drinking a beer. Whatever you feel for you is easy and attractive, whatever you feel you want to do, that is probably what will happen. But this is also about seeing that everything you do is it. Everything you do all day is the beloved saying, 'Come home'.

How can that be?

This game is set up by what you are, in such a way that the invitation is everywhere. 'In order to manifest,' you said, what I will also manifest is a sense of separation. In that separation there will be a longing to come home. So what shall I do about that? Oh right! I will make an invitation to come home – in fact, I'll make *everything* the invitation'.

Of course, it isn't really like that because that is a story. It isn't as though it's something that happened fifty million years ago this is constant; it is eternally this.

o o o

171

I really liked it when you said on Friday night that life is a miracle.

Yes, it is. Of course, in the game of separation, we tend to feel threatened and what we do is we try to create a womb, we try to get back to the womb. We build that womb and by doing that we try to make it known. The way to make this dangerous, alien world safer is to try and know it.

When we meet somebody and we fall in love, it is unknown and it is wonderful but it is also unsafe. So what we do is we marry. We fence someone in and make them known.

There was a man who had problems with his marriage and a friend of his advised him to go and see this wonderful relationship guru. So he went along and the guru just gave him a mantra. The man went back to his wife and started using the mantra, and after a few days things were starting to get better. After ten days it was really wonderful.

He met his friend again down in the pub and he said, 'This mantra is just wonderful, it's amazing!' His friend of course wanted to know what it was.

He told him, 'Every time I see my wife I say, "This is not my wife" '.

We always make everything known so that it becomes safe; and in the end it becomes dull. When I say to people 'Sitting on the seat is a miracle', they say, 'Why? That's not very important!' But we're walking around in this absolute miracle – everything we touch is the beloved. It's alchemy – the transformation of everything into gold.

The strange thing is that everything *is* gold – all that is being transformed is the perception. The perception that 'Everything is dull and frightening and I am separate from the wall' is the prison we live in. The alchemy is the transformation of that perception, to see that it is the beloved, wall-ing.

In the wall is everything – emptiness, stillness, unconditional love. There isn't anywhere that is not the source. There isn't anything that is not the source, including separation, including neurosis, including suffering. It is all simply the source appearing.

o   o   o

Does trying to understand the source get in the way?

Yes, but there is nothing you can do about that. All the time there is a feeling in that mind/body that there is something to understand, that is the way it is – until that drops away. People come to these talks and the mind goes, 'Yes, but what about …? Yes, but what about … ?' Until it just gives up. All the time there is a question there and a wanting to understand there will be a wanting to understand. Until there is nothing left. When there is nothing left, suddenly there is just this.

When you say 'just this', would you call it a vibration or energy?

You could call it energy. You could call it life. All there is is life. There is no one living a life – there is life. All there is is life apparently happening – only apparently.

o   o   o

You make me laugh.

Yes, it's all a crazy joke. When you think about the activities of religion and the activities of the seekers who go all over the world … What are they going around looking for? It's here! This is it! As you step on to the plane, the step is it. It's a joke – looking for that which already is. Including going to see Tony Parsons!

But it's good fun!

Oh, seeking can be good fun, though it isn't fun whilst you think it isn't fun.

The amazing thing about this is that there is only this; nothing has ever happened. There is no such thing as past or future. This contains within it all the apparent past. Everybody sitting in this room has a face that tells you a story about an apparent past; you can read people's faces. Though actually there isn't a past – there's only an apparent past.

The other amazing thing about this is that in this is the emptiness, the nothingness. When people talk to me about consciousness being at rest and then manifesting, I know it isn't like that. When I look at the wall, I see the rest and the stillness and the emptiness and the life altogether in one. There is everything in that. It can never be comprehended – it can only be seen, by no one.

That also means there is no cultural evolution?

No, but there is the appearance of cultural evolution, and that is all part of the dream. Mind is so powerful and it always wants there to be something called time; mind can only exist in something called time. So it creates it. It's genius! It creates the idea that there were dinosaurs and all the rest of it. There are scientists who can *prove* that this bone is, let's say, three million years old. There was a guy in London who said to me, 'I do have a past! Look, these are my children – here are the photographs to prove it!'

How come we are all committed to the same dream?

The strange thing – and this is another stroke of genius – is that actually we don't have the same dream. Every mind/body sees the wall as uniquely their wall. There is no one else in the whole of this apparent existence who sees the wall as you see it. That wall is *your* invitation. Words are inadequate … In a way, what I am saying is that we are all gods walking around in our own manifestation, believing we are separate people – until that belief drops away.

All the time there is a sense of separation, there is a sense of time, a movement towards somewhere. The great avoidance of presence is the idea that what you are looking for is over there. 'It can't be this – it isn't just this … Tomorrow morning at 6 o'clock yes, but not this. It *can't* be just this … Surely it's not just this?' That is the game.

o   o   o

Do you feel cold when your bare feet are on the ground?

Yes. I feel whatever you feel, but there is no one here who owns that. Everything can be felt in this mind/body. Anger arises, pain arises … anything you would like to name can arise in this, but there is no longer an ownership. There is no longer anyone who invites it to tea. It's not invested in – it's just there.

Liberation isn't about a separate person who is exclusive and doesn't feel pain. People may try to convince you of that but that's a misconception. The idea that an enlightened person walks around in something which is totally blissful is complete bullshit. It comes from either a deep ignorance or a wish to manipulate. It is the mind's idea of what perfection should look like, and it's nonsense.

People have the strangest ideas of 'how I will be when I'm enlightened', and sometimes I see the game that that body/mind is playing in order to avoid its own magnificence. I don't have a gift or anything – it's just that when I talk to somebody I can sometimes see the game they play not to awaken.

Can you tell us?

You would have to pay double! And anyway it wouldn't be any use to you because you wouldn't be able to do anything about it. If that is the game you are going to play, then that is the game you are going to play, until it drops away.

o   o   o

175

Since Friday there has been a sense of nothingness. It is still intellectual but …

Whatever works, works. There seem to be different ways in how this first manifests or appears. For a lot of people, first of all there is a sense of separation, strangely enough; it's another sense of being separate. It can seem almost as though there are two identities. One is the identity that you've apparently been walking around with for forty or fifty years. Then there seems to be another identity, which is called the watcher, the one that sees. This is the opening to the final adventure.

Isn't it all a concept?

If you close your eyes now … you don't have to, but if you want to, you can close your eyes and be aware of something in your body. There is always something happening in the body. Is that a concept? Or is it that you feel it and then the mind conceptualises it?

Yes.

So that is your invitation. What you are sees that that mind/body turns everything that happens into a concept. That's it. Don't try to do anything with it. More and more the seer emerges, the one that sees that. It doesn't matter what is seen – all that happens is that the seer sees. The seer is sitting there, seeing you seeing me. And has always been there. For all these years there has always been the seer, seeing you eating your dinner.

o   o   o

How do you deal with pain? I would think that it is easy for you to disconnect from the concept that there is pain.

There's no question of *dealing* with pain, but if there is a headache, I notice that this mind/body takes an aspirin. Not always, but sometimes. Just like anybody else. But there is no longer a sense of somebody owning something. Normally we feel something is wrong and we say, 'This is happening to me'.

And if you hurt yourself and you're bleeding, what do you do?

I do whatever you would do.

You wouldn't feel shaken up?

It hasn't happened for a long time. It's quite possible that if I were in a car accident, I would feel shaken up. But it wouldn't be *me* – it would just be shaking up arising.

o   o   o

Awakening simply happens – it has nothing to do with the apparent 'you'. So awakening can happen anywhere, in any situation. It can happen for some guy in the gutter down the road, high on pot or pissed on beer. Alternatively, there can be someone who is totally Zen, who has meditated for twenty years and who only eats watercress and in their case awakening *doesn't* happen. There are no reference points. Somebody who eats only watercress and meditates for twenty years can of course become awakened, but it wouldn't have anything to do with them eating only watercress and meditating – nothing at all.

I have friends who've meditated for twenty years and for whom nothing seems to happen.

What *can* happen is that they get totally fed up with it. They may not tell anybody else, they pretend they're still carrying on with it all, but deep down inside they've given up, or given up the motivation. And then – 'Oh!' – it happens. It's similar to what we are told happened to Buddha.

Would you say that my idea that I am here now because I have worked so long on my psyche is an illusion?

Yes. This is about the total dissolution of 'you', and everything that comes with 'you'. The idea of cause and effect is also displaced.

I've had a glimpse of what the Zen people call satori. Why does the glimpse go away again? What hinders it?

Nothing hinders it but there is still a sense of someone being there who saw something or glimpsed something, and who has then immediately gone back to what they think is their identity. The question 'Who am I?' can give people a glimpse of this, but in a way it's just another technique, and anyway it's an inappropriate question.

A glimpse of something through a technique is simply that – a glimpse of something through a technique. There is nothing about it that can last because there is no clarity. The lack of clarity lies in the fact that when people who have such a glimpse step back into what they think is them (the 'me'-ing as opposed to the being), they then think that they are in a different state that is not acceptable. That is ignorance. That's the difficulty with that sort of experience.

You'll notice that what I'm saying here is that there is nothing. And if you go on hearing this and somehow give up the idea that there is anything, then everything is possible.

This is only an appearance which seems to be happening in something called time. The mind is convinced that it's real. But all there is is this. Within the appearance is the apparent story, and you are the silence in which that apparent story arises. When that is seen – by no one – then what is apparently arising becomes a celebration.

Berlin
June 2002

You say that this can't be understood with the mind. Would you agree that my mind can understand that?

The mind won't understand the nature of one, and of course it can't understand why it can't understand the nature of one. The mind is simply another manifestation that comes out of one.

The mind is used to divide everything into two. It is out of the one that dualism arises, because the one is playing the game of two. This is what all this is about – you are the one, playing the game of being two. You live in this twoness and that is created through thought-form. This wall is a thought-form; the one uses the mind to create the appearance of wall.

But there is no way in which that tool can discover oneness. The tool is only part of the play. The mind is just a tool. Certainly the mind is useful in terms of coming to the realisation that it can't understand – but in the end, the mind just gives up. In a way, it longs to give up. The mind gives up looking and seeking, and then there is simply this.

All this is about is falling in love with this. Awakening is the dropping away of the one that is looking for paradise. When the looking for paradise ceases, it is seen that there is only paradise. The paradise is this *(rubbing the fingertips of each hand together)*.

Can my mind understand that it is possible to come here, for example, without seeking something?

Oh yes. In London, people who have dropped seeking and are now awakened (though I don't like that expression) come to these meetings. They still come and just sit there. They're not looking anymore – it's all over.

Can I be here without seeking anything?

There is nothing you can do about coming here or not coming here, by the way. But all the time there is what I call a 'me', there is a bereftness or a loss of something, a looking for something. All the time there is a 'me', there is a seeking, there is a longing. There can never be rest until it is discovered that I am the one.

It may be that the longing is not apparent, but as long as there is separation, there is only longing. There are plenty of people walking around out there who think they are not seeking, but they are all seeking the one. There is no one who isn't seeking – until there is no one.

Can one say that oneness is unconditional love and has created that?

Yes, absolutely. The one is unconditional love. There is only unconditional love, and there is the appearance of struggle and all the other things we see in the world, struggle and its opposite.

Unconditional love is not in any way connected with our idea of what love is. Christ said, 'I speak to you of that which is beyond the heart and mind of man'. There is no way we can know what this is. It is stunning; it is so stunning.

So it is futile to practise unconditional love in our state?

It is futile to practise and it is futile to try not to practise it. Just come to see that there is no one person practising … There is practising or not practising arising.

o o o

When you spoke yesterday about being intimate, I thought you meant, be intimate with whatever is now. So I thought it meant, if the agony is there, be intimate with the agony …

180

Hold on, there are two things here. First of all, there is the agony – but actually that is a story in the mind; that is a circuit, a tape-recorder. But there is also a feeling in the body of agony.

That's what I'm suggesting you be intimate with. Not in any fixed or focused way – simply seeing this. There is agony here … he's doing that … there's a car hooting … the wind's blowing through the window … there is agony here … there's a drink of water … It's simply letting those things be seen.

What is happening is stopping the world. What is happening is that there is a stepping out of the prison of individuality. It's like a prayer.

Awakening is the readiness to give up the struggle, the suffering; to give it all up for nothing.

o   o   o

In awakening, could you say it would not be possible to be dishonest?

It's beyond being honest or dishonest. Being is beyond any comparative thing. That's just the ignorance of the mind about how you should be. Being is beyond any sense of values.

My fantasy is that when there is awakening all these things are happening, but as if by some kind of magnetic force, there are more pleasant feelings than before.

No, not at all. What is there goes on being there, but there is the acceptance of those things rather than the investment in them.

The teaching that awakening is bliss is very attractive to the mind. There are these teachers who sit out in the front, usually high up, surrounded by photographs and flowers and candles … They move very slowly, and talk very slowly, and are apparently very blissful …

We long for that formula; we long to take the pill that will make us totally blissful and all our problems will be gone. It's the great con – the ticket to heaven! 'You can be like me – but you will have to work very hard and pay me a lot of money, or give me a lot of attention and a sense of power ...'

You've smashed my hopes! My hope was that if I totally feel something like jealousy and I don't avoid it, a time will come when it's gone.

No.

No hope?

No. When there is somebody there who says, 'I will be intimate with jealousy so that at some point or other it will go away', you are into another deal. You've got somebody there doing a deal with jealousy.

This is about losing yourself. This prayer of intimacy we're talking about is a readiness to give up the world for this. And *this* can be a deep feeling of jealousy. There is no question of jealousy going away – there is a readiness to simply see it.

Could you say that being enlightened is better for you?

No, because there isn't anyone. You always have to come back to that – there isn't anybody it could be better for. There is just life – as opposed to, 'I have a life that isn't very good and could be better, or is better at the moment but could be worse again'. That awful insecurity – 'My life is good but it could be threatened' ... All that goes, and there is simply life.

o   o   o

Does sexuality go away?

It's the first time sexuality actually happens. Of course, there's nobody there thinking, 'Is this going to work tonight or isn't it?' Sexuality is just celebrated.

182

Is it not a holy thing? Is it just ordinary?

All holiness falls away. There is no such thing as spiritual sex. There is just good old sex, multiplied by one hundred. Everything is sacred. The wonder is in the seeing.

So what is it with Barry Long, who says there is sex on the one hand and making love on the other?

I know some people who for years tried to make love spiritually and tried to push away the feeling that is sexuality. The moment the mind gets hold of an idea like spiritual love it gets holy. There is nothing wrong with lust – lust is wonderful, lust is life, it's aliveness. That's what is not seen. All those kind of teachings are dualistic – they're about a person having to conform to an ideal and they reinforce separation.

In his books it all sounds very nice, though.

Yes, but something else can be touched when you read the books. What is touched is the knowing that you are the one, and that actually in a way nobody can invade you in the freedom of oneness. It has nothing to do with the way you or anyone else makes love. I think what is touched in you is something else that is beyond an idea that there is a certain way to be. Don't forget, when dualism speaks to people, that teaching presumes incorrectly that there is a person who can choose to make love spiritually or not. I think you are touched by something deeper.

There is also a book of his about fear which touched me very much. Maybe you're right and I'm touched by something else, but I didn't feel he was talking to a person.

Except that there is that suggestion that there is someone who can choose. Whereas actually you are beyond choice – you are beyond everything. You are the source of all that is, including lust, and sexuality …

I've also read a book by Barry Long. I've forgotten most of it but I remember that he says that very often, when we have sex, we're not with the actual person but with a fantasy about the person. And he says that it would be good to return to the moment and really feel the other person.

Well, who chooses? Who chooses to be in the fantasy or not? There is no choice. What he is implying is that it is better to be with the person you are with than to be with the fantasy. He is presuming there is a person, and he is also saying, 'This is better than that'. That is dualism. If you want dualism, you can go and have a ball with teachers of that kind.

But I think what is touching you is that these people also point to something that is beyond what they are speaking about. What he is actually trying to impart is beyond what he is saying. We are talking about something which is totally beyond the words.

When you say 'This is it', I feel acceptance. But when you say 'It's all a dream', I feel a resistance and a lot of fear.

The dream is the idea that there is someone. That is the dream of separation. There is only this – that is not a dream, that is how it is. What you see in separation – for example, that the wall is separate from you – is unreal. You live in unreality. When there is no one, then there is living in the reality that everything is presence.

So we won't lose everything?

You can't lose anything – you never had anything. The whole idea of there being someone is 'I am here and I have things'.

But to give up everything doesn't mean to give up my normal life?

No, just give up the idea of anyone there having anything. You can't do it, but something in there hears this and it will happen.

When Christ said to the rich man 'Give up everything and follow me', he didn't mean a house or clothes. He meant, 'Give up the idea that you own or are anything'. You don't have to give up jobs or anything – you just give up the idea that there is anyone who has a job. Jobs are just happening to no one.

Some say, 'Give up sex – go beyond it'.

Oh, that's all ignorance. It's the mind's way of staying in the story. The mind wants you to stay in the story. The story then continues with a 'you' who is going to give up this and that.

When a teacher tells his people that they should be celibate, who is going to give up sex? Apart from the fact that no one ever was celibate. Monks may attempt to be celibate but life is not celibate. It's all nonsense but it's a story, and the mind loves a story.

Adam was walking around in the Garden of Eden feeling very lonely, so God asked him, 'What's the matter with you?' Adam complained that he didn't have anyone to talk to. God told him he'd give him a companion and it would be woman.

'This woman', he said, 'will cook for you and wash your clothes … She'll always agree with every decision you make. She'll bear your children and never ask you to get up in the middle of the night to take care of them. She won't nag you and she'll always be the first to admit she's wrong when you've had a disagreement. She'll never have a headache and she'll give you love and compassion whenever you need them'.

Adam asked, 'What's a companion like that going to cost me?' – to which God replied, 'An arm and a leg'. So Adam said, 'What can I get for a rib?'

o o o

You say we are living in a dream. Is Tony Parsons' dream the same as my dream?

185

The personal dream is uniquely your personal dream. You live in your own unique invitation. The dream that seems to happen is uniquely yours. All the time the invitation is there, it is uniquely for you. When the invitation is accepted, there is only this.

Is 'this' objective? What has often given me a strong fear is when I have the feeling, for example, that nobody sees a colour in the same way I do. That means to me that I am in my personal prison, completely alone.

You could call it a prison if you want. You are totally alone, yes. All the time you are separate you are totally alone. When awakening happens there is only one, so you are never alone there is just all-oneness. All the time you are separate, you live totally on your own. Nobody sees this wall like you see it. It is uniquely your world. It is there only to invite you to see that you are the one.

The only difference between you and me is that there is an idea in there that you are a person.

When I hear 'Drop the idea of being a person', I go totally blank. I mean how to do that?

Of course *you* can't drop it, but something inside registers that. Something resonates and says, 'Oh God yes, it's only a fantasy!' There is some sort of recognition there. I'm not suggesting for a moment that you can drop the fantasy, but even seeing that it is a fantasy is already the beginning of dropping it.

I totally agree with everything you say, except for this part – I feel that it doesn't really click. There is a seeing, and at the same time an utter non-comprehension.

It is something that is beyond any comprehension or imagination. Nobody in this room can conceive what it is like to drop there being 'me'. It's colossal. There has been a living for years and years with that 'me'.

Does awakening go together with pain in the body?

All the time there is a separate person, there is an idea of cause and effect. We might think a pain arises in the body because I'm worrying about my bank balance, so if I don't worry about my bank balance I won't have any pain in my body. It's all nonsense but it's what we believe. When there is no one, there is still pain in the body, there is still the overdraft ... They are simply what arises. There is no longer any identification.

o   o   o

What's meant by the rising of kundalini?

That's just the rising of what is believed to be kundalini. It's another belief system. It's an experience – like the experience of burning your tongue or eating chocolate. The experience of kundalini rising is the experience of kundalini rising.

Do I have this experience only because I have read about it or heard about it?

It possibly can happen without reading about it, but it has absolutely no meaning. No experience has anything to do with awakening. Awakening is the end of the one who experiences or seeks.

Can listening to this help us to awaken?

Well, nothing can help you because there is no one there to be helped. What can happen is that the concepts fall away and there is nothing left. It can cut through confusion.

But why are we meditating and listening to this and reading books when we actually cannot do anything?

Because you believe that you *can* do something. You think there is someone there who can choose.

But for the mind it's not clear that there isn't a person …

Oh no! The mind hates the idea that there is no person. The mind is the person. 'I am a person' is a thought. The mind doesn't want to give up the idea of its existence, or its apparent existence.

How then can I realise that I'm not a person, that I'm – let's say – a spiritual being?

You're not a spiritual being. You are nothing – and everything.

And fulfilled in this no-thingness?

No. It's got nothing to do with fulfilment.

o   o   o

I live a spiritual life …

You do? How awful! I forgive you!

I have a question about the body. I know the question is not very clear.

That's all right.

When you say not to identify … I do feel that I'm looking through the eyes of this body, that I breathe, that I eat …

Yes, the difficulty with this is that we think there is a location. 'I see through these eyes and there is this body, therefore there must be someone here; there must be something that is in this place'. If you look at it in another way and try to see that whatever arises is the beloved, whatever arises is the one … One of the things that arises is seeing from here, and another thing that arises is the body – let's say this body. That's the one arising as this body and this seeing.

It is difficult but it's actually the reality. The reality is that all there is is simply seeing. The mind makes up the idea that there is someone seeing. The mind takes possession of being and turns it

188

into an object called 'me'. There is simply a seeing of everything. Everything is this. There isn't anything else. I know that you apparently live in a house somewhere ... But actually all there is is this. There is always only this arising.

This is the one. This is the lover. Everything that arises is the absolute – including the seeing from what apparently is over there seeing this. The idea that it's over there is only an appearance. What is happening is that the one is seeing everything. And at the moment everything is, let's say, Tony Parsons moving his hand. I am everything. This is everything. You are everything. You are the one appearing as two. There is no location.

Something else in me says, 'Well, there is the planet earth ...'

No, there is no planet earth. There is no house you live in ... There only needs to be this, because this is everything. And when you walk into your house tonight, that is everything; it is the one. It's all the same thing – it just looks different.

I can totally understand your confusion – you think it's happening to you. You think you are walking around in a location called 'me', looking at things. But there is only the one being two. This room, your house – they are all only the one appearing differently. That is the miracle.

What's meant by the heart? Other teachers – like John de Ruiter often speak of the heart.

The heart has nothing to do with this. Awakening or oneness has nothing to do with any sort of location or any sense of the heart; it is totally beyond any idea of the heart. Also, the heart arises in oneness ... The problem with all of that sort of speaking is that there *is* only oneness. And when you get into ideas about the heart you get into ideas about something that is spiritual. It is a teaching that arises out of the devotional energy which has not yet been integrated with the impersonal.

o o o

I know this question has already been asked in another form, but if there is a realisation of being the one, what changes in life?

Nothing, except the perception.

I still have an idea of some miraculous change and that things go more smoothly, more easily.

Well, it just so happens that they do, but if that is the idea behind realising oneness, it will never be realised through that motivation.

But life must be very different if there is no judging anymore.

That certainly is the appearance that usually happens, but there is no guarantee.

What is your perception of your own body like?

There is a body – there is no perception of a body – there is just the body. I can only say to you that there is an awareness of a body-feeling which isn't anybody's. That awareness is no more sacred or meaningful than the awareness of sun shining through the window or drinking beer or hearing a car. They are all the one. There isn't anything closer or more special or meaningful about the body.

And when the body experiences pain?

When there is a headache there is a headache.

I still have a belief that when I include everything life is smoother than when I exclude.

Yes, that's so. But don't look for it. I can already hear the mind saying, 'If I can give up everything, I'll get something called harmony'.

I tried to become rich because I didn't want to be poor. It never worked ...

It *can* work – I've been rich. You can't say one thing happens for everyone. Again, it's the unique invitation. For you to discover that you couldn't get rich was the gift – an utterly beautiful gift. Everything that apparently happens for us is the gift, simply because oneness is absolute poverty and absolute wealth.

o   o   o

I've heard you say that awakening is being intimate with everything. There is no distinction between this body and that chair. It is one flow of ...

Life. Awakening or oneness isn't really being intimate – it is simply that everything is what it is.

Do you share your inner dialogue with your wife?

What do you mean by inner dialogue?

What you're thinking, what you're feeling ...

No, not always!

I do and I always get into trouble.

You are still trying to do something. You've been told you should be totally honest with your wife. It's a way of trying to make your life work. I'm not interested in that.

But if I tell the truth, I've got more energy.

'If I do this or that, then my energy will be clear and I'm winning again'. For God's sake, when are you going to give up trying to win? It is all such a meaningless struggle to become something else.

o   o   o

You talk about the one as being impersonal, but there are teachers -Ramakrishna, for example – who had a personal relationship with this impersonal being.

So he claimed. Relationship is between one and another. But there is only one. You can't relate to one because you already are one.

Maybe he was just trying to bring it down to our human level.

Oh God *(big sigh)* ... 'Maybe it's not that easy – maybe it's a big struggle. Maybe you should be like Ramakrishna' or whatever his name is. That's what the mind says. The mind is so attracted to this agony of never being good enough. You *are* the one. You are the divine expression. Nothing needs to change. Everything about that is totally perfect and always has been. It is beautiful. Nothing changes except seeing that you are the one. That's all. It's so utterly simple.

The idea of bringing something 'down to the human level' is generated directly out of ignorance and arrogance. The ignorance comes out of the presumption that the mind can and must understand something in order for awakening to happen – this is generated out of a deep ignorance. What is being communicated here is totally beyond the mind and heart. It is speaking directly to the wisdom we all already are.

It is far easier for an utterly simple person to see this than it is for a person loaded with the luggage of so-called spiritual knowledge.

Is awakening the end of suffering?

Let there be no dealing – you are trying to do a deal. Seekers do deals, finders give up dealing. There is always seeking whilst there is somebody who longs, who wants something. When the one that wants to give up suffering is no more, there is what is.

You don't have to do anything. You don't even have to

understand anything that is being said here. Just know that there is seeing. When you walk out of here, know that there is seeing; simply seeing what is.

What about karma?

The whole idea of karma and reincarnation and past lives even the idea that you have a past in this life – is a story. It's simply the reinforcement of that fairy story, the appearance of there being a past and a future.

You see, the mind is the tool that oneness uses to create two.

The mind's function is to divide and to live in time. It goes on reinforcing the idea that there is such a thing as time, or past lives ... Usually you were a great king – you didn't clean lavatories; you were a great healer or a witch ... It's usually pretty dramatic.

The idea of karma promotes the idea that you have lived before; you have acted in a certain way. In the appearance, it is what seems to happen, but it's all a metaphor, a parable. What you are living in is a parable. Cause and effect appear to be there; what appears in your life is that there is such a thing as cause and effect. And it seems real – no question about it. But all it is is the invitation for you to see that which is beyond the appearance.

Paul Lowe says, 'If you do this or that, it will have an effect'.

That idea has absolutely nothing to do with awakening. There is no connection, because he is presuming that there is a separate individual who has choice.

He's talked about being ordinary ...

What he is suggesting to you is that you should be ordinary. I'm not telling you that – I'm not telling you anything. What is being given to you is absolutely nothing. This communication is dissolving the idea that there is anyone there who can do anything. That is the parable; that is the story. And it's so convincing! Most people are totally convinced that this is real; that there is cause and effect. 'I am a real person!' In the dream it appears to be real, to the one who is separate. Awakening is simply the dropping of that idea. It's as simple of that.

I've tried all my life to be a good human being ...

Awful! It's so boring. Oh, the agony and struggle we go through in order to become something else! It is all utterly futile.

It has no effect?

No, no. That's the point, you see – nothing has any effect, except to disappoint. That is the gift. The lover that you are, the one that you are, is saying to you, 'Look, go on trying to be good and come to see that it doesn't work!' What it's saying to you is, 'You are the one'. That's the gift. It is all a gift, a beautiful, beautiful gift. It is all driven by unconditional love. It watches us rushing around looking for it, trying to be good ... And already there is only presence, unconditional love.

It's just so beautiful. I'm totally in love with this. I'm totally passionately in love with this. It's so amazing. It's so totally radical. It blows everything else apart, because it comes straight out of light and vanquishes the apparent darkness.

o   o   o

Can you say what you mean by the invitation?

The invitation is actually another part of the parable. There is an invitation but it is only the appearance of an invitation. Once the invitation card is accepted – by no one – then there is no invitation, because there is no one to invite. All the time there is a sense of there being someone who is searching for something, then what is being seen and touched and tasted is the beloved, the lover saying, 'You are already the one'.

The seeker lives in constant being. There never can be one moment where the seeker isn't invited. All of this is only the one, appearing as two, looking for itself.

What is invited?

Well, nothing is invited. But all the time there is somebody asking 'Who am I? What am I?' then the answer is everywhere. That is the game that's being played. There is only one. There is nothing else but one. You are one.

Does this exclude the idea that there is quite another dimension or world that is not included in this oneness?

No. If there is a sense of another world, then that is one arising as another world. But the thing about that is, why bother? Who wants another world? There won't be more oneness in another world.

This is you being the wall *(pointing at the wall)*. When there is no one, then that is simply seen. There is nothing magical or strange about that. The oneness is totally ordinary, and very natural. That is the way we are.

In a way finding it or not finding it doesn't matter, because there is nothing to find and there is nothing lost. When the body/mind dies and the mind ceases its function of dividing everything, there is just oneness. Now that can happen within the living body, which people call enlightenment; it always happens at death. When the mind ceases this function of splitting, there is oneness. So there's no hurry.

o   o   o

When I was five years old, it was so easy. I remember thinking about what would happen when I'm dead and I found myself in this space. Then I wanted to go back to my grandparents, and I came out of the space. There was no fear.

When this is a living thing, fear can still arise, though, because in the end there is no separate island here. Living in oneness there is an at-one-ness with everything, and in everything there can be fear as well. It's not a denial of anything – it's a welcoming of all that manifests. However, there is no longer anyone who is afraid.

○   ○   ○

Since I've been coming to listen to you, I've quite lost interest in becoming enlightened. I am still at the point where the 'I' doesn't want to disappear, so why become enlightened? The idea seems terrible. But what happens is that this not wanting to get somewhere has an effect on my life, what I do and where I go. I'm not so interested in going to see teachers because it's pointless.

That's great. Wonderful.

The other thing is that, after coming back from the retreat in Holland, there was a moment where I saw that what is looking through these eyes is the same as that which is looking through all these eyes. Sometimes that sense comes back and it's very exciting. So there is something happening, and at the same time this idea of 'me' is as strong as ever.

Let's go back to the beginning of what you said, because there might be a misunderstanding here. All that is dropped actually is the seeker, the one that is bereft, that is looking for something. There is no longer any question here of where it is, because this is it.

But you are not going to lose the character, that unique character. Not only will it still be there – it will be more celebrated; it will just blossom in that being. All that is really dropped is the one that is struggling to find something.

I don't know what you mean exactly when you say you don't want to drop 'me'. If you mean you, the character, you won't drop that. All of that will be a total celebration, because there is no longer a looking for something else. It's just the dropping

196

of the seeker. You don't need to come here, you don't need to go anywhere. Nobody needs anyone.

I don't feel I've got it.

That comes – really! Falling in love with trees, and with bus-stops …

When you say that, I notice there isn't even any anticipation. It's just so nice being here.

Absolutely!

o   o   o

My belief that I must do something to make things better goes so deep.

So go and see a therapist. What's wrong with that? It's absolutely perfect. Nothing is right or wrong. It only is what it is. If what is there is going to workshops and making life better, then that is what is there.

What is being communicated here is 'Relax! It's fine – why question?' I think modern therapy is the most intelligent thing around in trying to make one's life work. There's no doubt about it – it works, for a while … And it's fascinating because it's all about ME. 'I am really, really important, aren't I? In fact, my process is far more important than yours!'

o   o   o

Could you talk about aloneness or loneliness? Yesterday, after I left, I felt very strong, very much at one. Then after a while I was alone, and I could see the character coming in, with emotions, reactions … Barry Long said that the mind is like a dog and has to be kept on a leash. Either I do something to distract myself or those thoughts keep coming.

So what is it that sees that?

I see it, but it's so strong!

Yes that happens … But something in there sees that more and more. Once there is a seeing that there is nothing that can be done about it, then a totally new world opens. All the time that you are convinced that you can do something about that character coming back, that mind that needs to be kept on a leash – all the time that is there, there is somehow a sense of a will. When you let go of that, then a whole new world opens.

Just go on letting go.

When Tony Parsons walked across the park and then there was no Tony Parsons, one of the senses that came with that was total aloneness. There was a sudden seeing that what I saw was not normally seen. I couldn't go to someone else and say 'You are the one' – they would have taken me to the local mental home.

In a way everyone is alone, actually. In separation we are alone and feel lonely as well, because we can't really reach anyone. You're never going to know how green my table is – that's part of the parable. After awakening, there is no question of loneliness because there is only one and all.

That doesn't then mean that I could be you, or could invade what you are. I don't need to anymore. I don't need to invade anything or get anywhere anymore. I am in the paradise – I am the paradise.

So if I understand it rightly, you feel you are the one. That sounds rather abstract.

To the mind it sounds abstract, but it's more real than anything else. It is the only real thing, the oneness. Whilst we are separate we live in an abstract world; we live in a world of escaping life. Therapists say to me, 'Aren't you talking about avoiding life?' They think I'm talking about something called detachment. This has nothing to do with detachment. This is about being life in the most intimate, fullest way. In separation, we do live in an abstract world; we live in this thought world. In naturally being at one, there is nothing abstract. It is very immediate, very direct. It is being in love with this. There is nothing else but this.

I think it's got to do with the impersonal. For the person, the impersonal is totally cold.

Yes, it does seem like that. 'See the face of God and be disturbed' – as if it doesn't have any connection with love or life. But the impersonality in some way needs to be part of it, because the impersonality is to do with the freedom. There are no longer any hooks in anything. Life is just life. That is where the nature of impersonality comes in. There is no longer any sense of one thing being right and the other being wrong. Everything is just what it is. This has to do with freedom, with liberation, and also with the unconditional nature of love.

○   ○   ○

Where does fear come from?

It just arises. Where does a tree come from? Everything arises from one. Fear comes from nothing. It seems for the mind that fear comes with a story about 'She doesn't love me' or whatever. That is actually only a story. The actual fear is alive – the story is just information.

I thought fear arises because I am separate.

Yes, separation is the root of fear, but when there is no one, there can still be fear. When there is no one, then that no one is everything and lives in an appearance where fear arises. Let's also be clear that even after awakening, a sense of separation can still arise, but it has nothing to hold on to so it leaves again.

○   ○   ○

I know a teacher who praises people when they are able to watch and scolds them when they've gone into old habits.

That is the practice of pure dualism. You can be quite happy here, because I have no interest in you at all, and I see there is no one there who can choose.

Awakening brings with it the embodiment or the marriage of the polarities, which is liberation. What is happening more and more these days is that people have a glimpse and then they rush out and become gurus. The whole thing hasn't yet been embodied. 'Wisdom is knowing that you are nothing – love is knowing you are everything'. Now if you stay in the wisdom, there is still a subtle 'me' there. What it wants is for something outside to complement it, to feed it. There is an investment in proving something; there is a subtle 'me' that wants something. All the time that is there, there isn't the clarity; there's an investment in what's going on.

I have no investment in what's going on at all. I feel just the same sitting here as I do sitting in my garden at home. It doesn't matter if somebody wants to stay in therapy and make their life work – that is what is arising; that is the divine expression. There is nobody here in the slightest bit interested; there is nobody here who wants that any different. Here, there is an in-loveness with what is.

The whole implication of the sort of teaching you're talking about is that there is somewhere to get to. I'm not interested in you becoming anything, because you are already that.

o   o   o

Do you sometimes complain?

Yes, especially if the coffee isn't hot enough. When we stay in hotels, nearly always when they bring the coffee in the morning it's not hot. Even in Germany! In England you can understand, but

200

Germany – it ruins my whole day!

One of my concepts for a better life is to not complain.

Hold on – let's just stop there. Isn't the mind wonderful? Yesterday you said to me that one of the things you also believe in is being totally honest with your wife and that it has got you into the most awful trouble. So yesterday it was being totally honest. But today, when the coffee comes and it's not hot, you just drink it – and that is not being honest – because one of your other beliefs is that you shouldn't complain. It's all a silly contradictory nonsense. When your wife runs off with the milkman are you not going to complain or are you going to be honest?

I've paid so much money for all of this – honesty, not complaining …

Yes, I can imagine.

o   o   o

I've heard you say that when someone wakes up it is very helpful for the world; it brings light. That touched me very much.

If there are apparent people seeking in the world, and they apparently meet someone else who actually is nothing, then they expand into that. In general terms, in the overall sense of everything, there is no difference. But all the time there is a seeker who asks, then being with someone who is nothing is a way in which there can be an expansion. Because what they see is their original nature. What they see is what they are. A letting go of this tightness can happen.

There can be an escape in going out and helping others. That can be simply another avoidance of discovering that you are nothing. When oneness is embraced or embodied, there is no question of helping anybody – there is nobody who needs help.

o   o   o

With my two-year-old daughter it seems to me that I can clearly see how she has a feeling and then makes up a story to fit with it.

She is already separate, obviously.

Yes, there is a strong sense of 'me' and 'I want'.

Gorgeous. I've had four kids and they get into total ego-building. They were monsters – I could have shot all of them! It's playing the game of separation. 'I am separate and now I'm going to be *really* separate, the most important separate person in the world!'

o   o   o

Isn't it that to become more joyous and juicy in life I have to be more vulnerable?

Oh, this is another one now! First it's being honest, then not complaining – and now it's being more vulnerable. It's all about ways you 'should' be. Who is going to be that way? There isn't anybody, so how can anybody become vulnerable?

o   o   o

Can you say something about marriage, male/female relationships, what they are for?

In a way, you can say that everything is the invitation, but one very powerful situation is the man/woman or man/man or woman/woman relationship. But let's say, for the sake of simplicity, the man/woman relationship – which is only another appearance. What is powerful about it is that in some way or other it very strongly represents what we're talking about. What we're talking about here is the marriage, the final marriage, of male and female energy into one.

You could say that falling in love is the nearest thing you can get to tasting oneness. Falling in love – which for me is even

202

beyond sexuality – is like an adoration. There is a sense of losing oneself. All that exists is the beloved. After that you want to relate to that person, and then sexuality and all the other things come in. When you make love to someone, then what can happen is again you can lose yourself for a moment; there is no real recognition of you being a woman and me being a man. In that sort of energy awakening can happen.

Sexuality is so powerful, so to do with life; it represents the creation of life. The difficulty is that the mind keeps going back to me relating to you, and keeps on making you the object and me the subject. 'You are the person I'm going to relate to and you are over there and I'm here'. What is missed is that actually there is no relationship between you and me; there is no space between you and me. Actually you are me and I am you.

The meeting of male and female represent the meeting of ice and fire. Both elements extinguish each other and turn to vapour, and then there is nothing. This is the nothing of liberation – the final marriage which is beyond gender, beyond the apparent dualism of male and female.

One thing I've noticed with people looking for enlightenment is that the masculine energy wants to live in ivory towers or go into what I call a glass box. They want to become pure awareness and watch objects arise and see them fall away again. And the one thing they are absolutely terrified of is the female energy, because what they are really scared of is intimacy; being burned in the fire of intimacy. It's what I call a masculine trait, to want to be in that cold place.

That's why religion is anti-sex and anti-women, mainly because the religious influence has been patriarchal. Basically, the masculine energy is afraid of the fire of life. And the female energy is afraid of impersonality … So there's the marriage of what appears as a polarity.

Let's be clear about this, however – people don't have to relate in a heterosexual or homosexual way, or indeed at all, for this fusion to take place, simply because all of the elements of male and female are within each person.

o   o   o

For me it was important to discover that everything I do is a deal; everything I do has a purpose. The tendency to look for a meaning is very strong.

Once we become separate we are conditioned to protect ourselves from this alien world we dream we are in. The whole way we do everything after that is in a way to make deals. We live in this world of 'What can I get from this?' or 'How does this threaten me?' In separation, we put on one side our innocence, our childlikeness … We become business people.

But we need to do that. The whole of the drama is to lose the paradise in order to regain it. Previously, when there was paradise, there wasn't necessarily a knowing of that.

o   o   o

What does it mean when you say that me looking at you is myself looking at myself?

I can't tell you … It's indescribable, but it's very ordinary and natural. One of the difficulties that people who come to these talks have is that they walk around looking for oneness, thinking that it's something very magical and special and everything will shift … It's not like that. It's almost as if something goes away, which is twoness. What goes away is separation. To stay separate needs energy; you have to work at it. Every morning when we wake up we reconstruct 'me'. That's why we are so worn out at the end of the day.

Does silence have to do with the absence of thought?

It's the silence that sees the thoughts. Stillness is not stillness of the mind – stillness is that which sees that there is thought. You could say that everything emanates from silence. Silence is absence and needs nothing. Thoughts arise out of silence and fall back into silence … this is the manifestation of oneness.

Encinitas, USA
September 2001

It's good on a day like this to drop any expectation about anything. It's good really to withdraw totally that guy who sits there and wants things, wants to get something. If there can be a movement back – just a slight movement back away from any idea that anything's going to happen; if there can be just the sitting in this, then that's what can be most valuable in this sort of setting.

I won't give you anything – you don't need anything. You are sitting in everything – you *are* everything. It's just that, for some of you, there is the belief that that isn't the case; there's some idea you don't get it. But *you* never will get it – it's not you that's going to get it. When you're out of the way, then there it is.

It's always there – the love and the being are always present. That's what runs this whole manifestation – being. There is only being, and there are mind/bodies carrying that being and believing they are separate individuals. And believing that as separate individuals they need to get something, something needs to happen – some sort of explosion. And that after the explosion, everything will look different and all the feelings of frustration and fear will simply evaporate.

That's not how it is. Fear can still be here, and anger ... Anything that seems to happen in the world, in this apparent world, can still be in this mind/body – simply because it is in everything. I am everything, I am all that is, and all that is includes any anger that arises anywhere in this being.

So enlightenment or awakening has nothing to do with personal attributes – the dropping of desire, the dropping of the ego. That's just traditional nonsense. The dropping of thinking … Thinking can happen here, the ego can happen here, anything can happen here, because this is unconditional love. This is totally neutral. This is liberation. This embraces everything. I embrace everything that arises, I am everything that arises – everything. There can't be any exclusion, there's no denial. In awakening there is no denial – everything is embraced by the lover, everything is embraced intimately by the lover. Everything that arises is the lover and the lover embraces the lover.

You don't need anything from me because you are the lover, and whatever is happening in that mind/body for that mind/body is the beloved. Always the apparent seeker is in invitation – always in the invitation to see that you are the one; that you are the light that allows this creation to be.

There's nothing that can be done because there's no one to do anything. Awakening is simply the realisation that there is no one; there is no separate individual. The illusion of the separate 'me' drops away and there is what already is – what always is – the one constant lover, the one, the absolute.

So what is happening here is actually very ordinary; what is available here is very natural and simple. It's as simple as sitting on a seat.

In sitting on a seat, let there just be sitting on a seat. There's no one sitting on the seat, but sitting on the seat is happening. Seeing is no one seeing – there's just seeing. Hearing – no one's hearing; there is just hearing. All the senses are just happening; they are all the beloved's invitation. So let there just be seeing, let there just be hearing, let there just be sitting on a seat. Let there just be feelings – feelings of boredom, feelings of frustration … Let there be thoughts – 'I don't get this', 'What's this guy talking about?' Let that be there – that's all the beloved, it's all the invitation. There is nothing which isn't the invitation for the apparent seeker.

You live in total invitation, constantly. You can never get away from the tiger, you can never get away from the beloved. You can't escape what you are, which is the source of unconditional love. You are the absolute, you are the source, you are the nothing from which everything arises. And everything includes that body/mind, that person you thought you were, or you still think you are. It includes that idea that there's an individual there. The drama of this manifestation is only the search to discover that there's no one.

Once that's seen, then that's the beginning of the great adventure, that's the freedom, and then it expands ... At first it's seen that I am the awareness that arises, and then something else is embraced, something else is integrated, and then there is no longer any identification of any sort. There is only that which is beyond words.

So Tony Parsons doesn't live in awareness or constant mindfulness or constant anything. There's nothing happening anymore – just life, being life, with no question about that, with no judgement of it.

We're not talking about detachment – what we're talking about here is a love affair. Simply sit back and don't expect anything, and the lover will appear.

It's like walking through a jungle with a great big machete called 'becoming' or 'endeavour' or 'expectations', hacking down all these leaves that are in the way to find a way through to somewhere. And you go on and on, hacking at all the leaves, with this great sense of endeavour and expectation. You become totally exhausted and you drop to the ground and give up. And out of the woods comes a deer and kisses your nose.

It's very simple and it's totally immediate. It's right here. It is all there is.

If anybody wants to ask anything, we can now discuss this as friends together.

o   o   o

The fact that there is just awareness – in the way that I hear it, that's totally neutral. It's just this blank, it's awareness – so what? But then at the same time – and my own experience seems to validate this – when that nothingness is kind of just let be, this amazing love does come through. So there is something that's called love, that's not just awareness ...

And what is love? Is it some kind of energy? Is it an obligation? Obligation is the wrong word, but is it a force that wants to happen; that isn't happening because it's twisted or misconstrued or something? You know what I'm trying to say?

'Absolute wisdom sees that I am nothing; absolute love sees that I am everything'. (Those aren't my words.) Everything is generated from unconditional love – all of this is only unconditional love manifesting as a wall or a flower or a candle. This is unconditional love, candle-ing. You are unconditional love, Bill-ing or Joe-ing or whatever (that's to say, that body/mind is). All of that is generated from a totally liberated unconditional love – which is beyond our normal concept of love, which tends to be needy, which tends to want things and need things.

This love is totally radiant; it fills everything. But it also is neutral in the sense that it allows everything. It's a totally liberated love which allows any manifestation. Nothing can be except in that love, including Hitler, or whichever baddy you have in your head.

And certainly awakening is totally beyond just the idea of awareness. Certain people teach that awakening is the seeing that there is no doer; that consciousness is all there is. But there's something that *knows* that consciousness is all there is ... is the lover ... is the ultimate ... is what you are. There's a stuckness in that idea of just awareness. Something still hasn't blossomed unconditional love.

o   o   o

I'll take a risk here and speak for most of us where ego's still arising, while you're on the stage speaking from an awakened perspective, as you tell us. My question is, I know there is nowhere to go, as you say, and no one to go anywhere, but how does one lift that veil, so to speak?

You can't, you never will. You can't lift the veil because the veil is the idea of 'you'.

How does one drop that?

One doesn't drop it – but it's dropped by a seeing that there is no one. There is no one. There is no one there – there's just, if you like, space in which things apparently are happening (only apparently).

It's getting a sense of moving behind that guy who's always been around – you know, that apparent guy who's always been around ... And just behind that apparent guy who's always been around is the one who knows that guy standing there looking at me. You know that; you know that there's something just behind. Everyone in this audience knows there's something just behind watching them sitting there looking at this. Incidentally, what's happening here is that you are listening to you. It's me speaking to me, and something in there knows this.

So practice is futile? Any sort of practice?

Who's going to practise? Who's going to practise – the guy who's going to get there? 'I'm going to go on practising until I get there ...' And so he is constantly in a state of 'getting there'. But where is he trying to get to? There is nowhere to go. This is it, as it is. Practice only reinforces the sense of me practising. It is the

210

spiritual ego at work.

But it seems to me that the opposite of practising would be to just carry on like everybody else ... You know, the great majority of the people in the world out there are just going about their ways, their ego ways.

Absolutely, it's the purest meditation. In a way everybody is searching. They're all out there looking for something, whether they think it's wealth or whatever you like. Actually, really what they're looking for is this. Everyone is a seeker, but once there's a recognition that what you're looking for is beyond you, then there's a readiness to die.

Then there's a tremendous relaxation and you can just stand the way you're standing and be the way you are and nothing has to change – it's absolutely divinely perfectly appropriate. The way you are is exquisite. It's a total change of perception. It's not about – oh, you know – 'I could be better' or 'I have to change' ... It is totally around the other way, in seeing that what you are is totally exquisite – just as it is, with all the neuroses and problems that body/mind thinks it has. That is the unique way it needs to be.

I appreciate what you're saying, I really do, but one thing I would like to say about it is that for Tony Parsons, before you realised that there's this empty space, you were on some sort of a search, you were looking ... I mean, from what you say in your book and some other things I read ... I don't know if you would call it a practice, but you were seeking, you were looking, right? There was kind of a quest for 'What is this life all about?' And that's different from your average Joe Schmoe who's out there doing whatever.

It's the final step that's taken ... I mean, most people live their lives without, let's say, seeking enlightenment. At death, of course, they find what they've always been seeking all their life, because they've never moved away from it. But in life, when there's a seeking for the final resolution, yes, it is the final seeking – but it's all the same seeking. It's only that you've refined it down to the final search (which, incidentally, is the death of 'you' – that's the final realisation, that there is no 'you'). But that seeking out there is just as sacred as this seeking in here. There's nothing more worthy about this as compared to that – it just feels more worthy, to be a seeker for enlightenment rather than wealth.

o   o   o

It seems that from the body/mind reference point there are emotions, the whole range of emotions that arise, and there's an observer there or there's a witness – or rather, there's a witnessing, a watching of this occurring. But is it that there are different levels to this, a deepening or a refining of the recognition … ?

OK, so as far as I'm concerned, observation is still to do with the mind. For me, the word 'self-observation' is simply the mind watching the mind, or the mind watching what seems to be happening. It has no relationship to awakening at all, because usually in self-observation there's some sort of judgement or analysis of what's happening, and the need to change that. That has nothing to do with liberation -it has to do with manipulation.

Impersonal watching is another phenomenon that takes place when somebody is opening to the discovery of their original nature. First of all, there seems to be a watcher – that's why I suggest to people that there's something behind them watching them sitting there looking at me. That in a way is certainly the first opening for many people.

So that's like an all-inclusive type of watching?

Yes, but that falls away also. Just as the invitation falls away in the end. Once the invitation is accepted, there's no need for an invitation. So the watching and the invitation are in a way, you

212

could say, preliminary steps or preliminary happenings (that makes it sound like a process but it isn't) that seem to arise when there's an opening to the realisation of our original nature.

For me, Tony Parsons, when watching used to be there, it was somewhere sort of up there *(pointing behind the head)*. For some people it's all over the body; for other people it's in the head. It's a simple seeing of what is arising without any need to change it. It's the first beginning of awakening. It's the initial sense of impersonality.

OK, and in that beginning of awakening, as one deepens in that contentment, does the personality experience emotions? Is there a level of deepening where those don't even arise?

No, they do arise. We're coming back to the fact that it has nothing to do with individualism. Emotions arise in this body/mind. I have to say that for this body/mind they don't have the drama, there's no great charge to them anymore – there is simply an emotion that arises and lives for a few seconds and then is no more. But let's be clear about this – emotions arise because I am this, I am that. It's not to do with the individual – it's to do with the whole of manifestation. And at the moment, for this body/mind, the whole of creation is this. This is the creation there isn't anything else – nothing else exists.

So, to be a bit more specific, is there a charge that arises as one deepens?

When you say a charge, there is an energy in the emotions or feelings have a charge … It depends what you mean by charge.

Like a hook to …

No.

A charge that would create a contraction.

Oh, contraction can happen, yes. But that only is there – and then not there. Nothing can live for very long in this. There's no

213

one there who's taking delivery of it. I keep on having to come back to this thing that awakening has absolutely nothing to do with this individual. I am not liberated ... And if somebody tells you they are liberated, walk away, or just say 'Yeah sure, and I'm Shakespeare'. It's meaningless. There is only liberation, there is only light, this is the light. I don't see anybody here – I only see being in the form of apparent people. There's nobody here.

○   ○   ○

You mentioned a sort of apparent sequence that different people go through. You were intimating that something starts, and then something else unfolds, and it grows into more ... something else appears that has more dimensionality to it or fullness to it or something like that. You mentioned also the way the opening began for you. My wife had a similar sort of experience, of watching it behind the head.

For different people it's always going to be different, so I'm reluctant to ask this question, because you don't want to go through a sequence that sets up a projection. But I find it very helpful in the transitions we go through to get a sense of the kind of stages that go on, in a general sense – that it starts one way; there are certain indications; it enriches somehow within itself; the flavour of it changes, the tone of it changes, the scale of it changes somehow ...

Yes, certainly so far as Tony Parsons is concerned, there was a sense before walking across the park of this watcher which suddenly seemed to appear. I seemed to be doing things and there was this guy watching – this impersonal watching, just watching. It was totally impersonal – frightening in a way, a bit frightening, a bit strange, because of its impersonality.

Did it seem like there were two of you?

Yes, in a way – the watcher and me.

Both were in sort of equal balance?

No, the watcher was totally greater than me, than my sense of 'me'. Don't forget that for me this whole thing began in Christianity. I didn't last very long in the Christian tradition (that's another story), but basically in a way there was a sense of God watching. But that soon fell away when I came to realise there was no such thing as God.

And I do notice with other people (this obviously being more in London and so on) that there are people there who are no longer people. Awakening has happened, and I see that beforehand for some of them there was a sense of a watching ... But it's uniquely different for each person. (Certainly the way they describe that opening is different.)

For some people there's a noticing first of all of an increase in what they would call neurotic behaviour. Once there's an opening to dropping the 'me', then the 'me' comes in and fires with all guns – for some people, not for everyone. But I do get people phoning up and saying, 'God, my worst fears are now happening! What's going on?' So that seems to be a part of what goes on.

The other thing that seems to go on with people is the desert. Obviously, what we are talking about here is a total devaluing and desolation of any ideas or concepts we have about our own lives and the value they have. Let's be very clear about that – so far as I'm concerned, nobody here has a life. Nobody's life is ever going to work – that's the whole idea of this. We think we have a life that's going to work, or we're going to try and make it work – it never ever does. That's the whole thing – having an apparent life is about deep disappointment. That's the invitation, that is the love. Become disappointed and then you look somewhere else.

Quite a lot of people come to my talks in London and they keep on coming – which is the only thing I would recommend in a way, people coming and hearing this ... Because the mind goes on saying 'Yes but ... Yes but ...' And then gives up; it just gives

215

up. So for quite a few people they go into a desert because they lose the sense they had of the value of their own life. They actually lose hope – there's no longer any hope that it's going to get better or that they can make their lives work. They give it up.

So for some people – again, not for everyone – there's a period of walking through a desert (rather like Christ in the desert, really), where they've lost their old life, the scaffolding has fallen, their old life is no longer there. They don't have any values anymore, they've got nothing to get excited about – and they haven't yet fallen in love. There are quite a few people in London, in England, walking around in a desert ... also in Holland that's happening.

It's not always the case, but for quite a number of people that is a part of what happens – and they phone me up and complain! All I can say to them is, 'Just go on just being intimate with this, with whatever ... Just see what is, and then the falling in love begins to happen'. There isn't anything else, there's nothing else, there isn't any hope ... There's only this – really. And there's always only this.

o   o   o

It's been useful to have some of your phraseology in As It Is *to help release the idea of the person. For instance, the idea of the divine expression, or the manifestation of consciousness, somehow helps release ownership ... I was wondering if you could say something about the bringing of heart into this desert, about being intimate with what is.*

One of the difficulties that apparent people have with approaching the beloved or awakening is what could be called the male approach to it. (And I am not referring to gender. There is no such thing as a man or a woman – there are just some body/minds that have a leaning towards a more masculine approach, and other body/minds that have more of a leaning towards a feminine approach.)

The difficulty with the more masculine approach is that it tends to come from something that's quite dry, to do with understanding, and there tends to be a huge investment in the idea of awareness. Somehow the idea of just being pure awareness has a feeling of safety about it – 'I can be safe in being awareness and letting things arise. I don't have to be involved in anything anymore. I never have to be involved in any sort of intimacy. I can be cold in my glass box of awareness and let things arise. This is the final liberation – at last I'm free of having to be alive'.

And to a certain extent we are conditioned by that traditional teaching, which has been around for many thousands of years, which comes from the male view of purity and abstinence and dryness.

It certainly isn't any fun.

No, it isn't fun, but it is very attractive, whilst one wants to stay safe. Whereas liberation is actually a marriage of detachment and devotion.

There is that clarity, that beautiful clarity, which tends to have a masculine sort of feel about it. There's something clear and beautiful and exquisite about that clarity … But it doesn't have the earthiness of the feminine; it doesn't have the earthiness of love, of deep intimacy, of real mixing in the mud. It's only partial, it's only a partial thing, and it needs to be married with the intimacy.

So when there's a feeling of being in this arid desert, then I suggest to people that they start to become very intimate with standing there feeling the body, opening to what's going on in the body, becoming soft and malleable and letting the sweetness of that present happening invade the being, invade the awareness so that that whole side of awakening can come in.

Afterwards, of course, it's all over – there's no longer one thing being stronger than the other. It's being ready to wonder at the unknown; it's the excitement of the unknown in life that we begin to wonder at. That's what it feels like.

Thank you.

This is very very sexy, you know. Awakening is very sexy.

Isn't this what tantra teaches?

Yes, tantra was the first religion. Well, it was the first, let's say, idea that unfortunately became organised. Brilliant ideas, radiant ideas become organised and become religions and become dead. This is about tantra, yes.

It's like the monk who went to work in the monastery where they were writing out all the scriptures. He had to go and write them and translate them too, but he noticed that the monks were translating from copies of the original text. They weren't translating from the original text – they were translating from copies of the original text. And he thought there could be a mistake in the copies, so he asked the master if he could go down into the dungeon or the cave and go back to the original scripture or text.

So he did that, and about two days later people noticed he was missing. They went down and there was this monk, crying his eyes out. They said 'What's up?' And he said, 'I've been reading through these original scriptures and I've suddenly seen that the word is not "celibate" – it's "celebrate"!'

I think the difficulty with things like tantra is that the mind gets hold of the idea that it can find God through sex, and then that becomes another 'way'. What's not seen is that we are always in sexual intercourse, we're always in this intimacy. This intimacy, this beloved never leaves us. The beloved is always enveloping us, metaphorically. We're always in that love, always.

With some of the Tibetan forms of tantra, the love is the constant contact with the energy of life and the sexual part is nothing special at all,

218

because everything is that, and so it's just a total opening to life.

In a very ordinary way.

○ ○ ○

Last night you were talking about the value of meditation – primarily that if you did it long enough, you would get bored. What I was wondering is just what you meant by getting bored – that you quit trying to attain anything or change yourself somehow? You just accept ... Well, things just happen as they do and you don't try to do anything about that?

Yes, well, with meditation what you're trying to get to is some state of being, of behaving. You're trying to work your way towards ideas of how you could be ... And you never will. There is no one who can choose to accept or resist, just as there is no choice about formal meditation. In reality, everyone in the world is meditating.

Accepting life as it is?

Well, they try not to, but that also is a divine expression; the resistance to life is also the divine, resisting life. There is no formula. Meditation – or not meditation – will not bring anything at all. Acceptance of life – or non-acceptance of life – will not bring anything at all. The realisation of utter helplessness – and beyond utter helplessness, the beginning of the ending to the idea that there is someone standing there – that is what can happen.

But you can't do that; no one can do that. No one can do anything because there is no one to choose.

And that's what you meant by being bored through meditation?

Yes, it is a giving up of the idea that this guy can do anything.

The giving up of everything – that just happens? Nobody does it?

Yes. I think a part of that is also the coming to see that exactly what you are and what you appear to do is the invitation. You

219

don't need to do anything. The way you get up off the seat and walk out of the room and get into your car; the way you eat your lunch; the way you breathe; the way you meekly sit there and look at the sky – that is it. And so it is being done. You know, you can sit in your kitchen with a cup of coffee and think, 'All right, I'll go upstairs to my sacred altar with the candles and meditate'. What the hell – the kitchen table and the cup of coffee is sacred! It is oneness being a table and a cup of coffee.

o   o   o

Tony, what do you mean by balance, how things balance each other?

The world as it appears to be is in total balance. It is totally neutral. It isn't good and it isn't bad. It is an appearance which is unconditional love appearing. Unconditional love is totally neutral; it is open and neutral and all-accepting. And so it presents the world – an apparent world – to apparent people. The people think it is a great series of happenings which have a meaning that will lead them somewhere. They think that their lives have some sort of purpose, and that each thing is a lesson about God's teaching. 'God has done it to teach me that I should become a better person', or whatever. It is meaningless. It is just a meaningless appearance that is perfectly balanced.

You said earlier that all the dark side of life – you know, the wars and craziness on television and stuff like that – is balanced by what is happening by the world sort of waking up.

There is a balance of negative and positive energy.

How does that work?

It is an exquisite work of genius. It is the most incredible happening there is. It is the manifestation of the absolute, the one appearing as two.

You may say it's a perfect world in perfect balance, but what with the

220

Middle East and all the other conflicts nowadays, what we get is the idea, the feeling, that the balance is off-balance, and weighted towards the dark side. And if you're actually living in Israel, you really believe that.

I think if you are living anywhere you live in fear. Once there is a sense of separation, then you live in what seems to be an alien world. There is no one who isn't afraid. All fear is primarily generated from the sense of separation.

o   o   o

I can hear you saying that the experience of awakening is in the ordinary and it's very simple. But the understanding of it ... it's very complex. Or at least, for my mind, it seems that it requires a refinement and almost a different or some very specific intellectual ability to deconstruct all the things and ...

No, not at all. It is actually about open childlikeness. Awakening is about simplicity. And what can happen before, with understanding, is simply the dropping of the concepts that one's mind has taken on board about the nature of life. What happens at these meetings is that people's understanding is dissolved.

There are your own concepts that you have already taken on board, and because they are generated by the mind, they always become complex – look at the religions. You then hear other concepts about those concepts – which can break them up again. Once the understanding is there, then the ideas you had just fall away. Eventually all understanding drops away and all that is left is this.

o   o   o

I'm from Brazil; I come from a third world country. And I think one of the things that really struck me about the Inner Directions gathering is how many white people there are. I've been in America for five years, and my previous experience was being a Christian in Brazil. So my experience

221

with spirituality has been a very mixed one. Church in Brazil is like the beach – it is poor and rich very much together; educated and uneducated together. And that is what Brazil is. The slums are right next to the rich.

So I guess where I am coming from is, do you feel that this message can be felt (I know it is about feeling) by people who share a different life experience in terms of their intellectual ability, in terms of their education, in terms of … ? That's my question. Because in America I only see it happening in this elite. Have you had experience with people who come from a different background?

There is somebody in London who came to me, and who is now doing his own teaching. He's a gardener, he comes from a working-class family. He had at some point done a lot of searching and conceptualising about this, but in the end what he came back to was what is a natural way of being, something very simple, something very childlike. He came back to his own childlikeness, his own sense of wonder, and dropped the pretence of being a separate individual.

This message is known by everyone. Everyone knows this. This is totally simple and totally immediate and totally direct. It will possibly take time for some concepts to fall away, but we don't have to have any concepts about it at all. What is shared here is beyond all understanding and beyond even the heart. It is also beyond all class or financial barriers. If there is a readiness to hear, it will be heard.

o   o   o

How can I communicate this? How am I ever going to tell anybody what this is? Because you can't communicate this, there is no way it can be communicated, and yet it is the most wonderful, simple gift there is. There is nothing else worthy of this; there is nothing else that even comes near this.

And so that is the passion, really. You know, the passion is expressed in the words in the book. I tried to write a book that was very simple and very to the point and that wouldn't confuse people. Actually, the strange thing is that it is not very good, that book; there is still the possibility of being confused by that book.

What I find is that this is in a way for me the most wonderful part – talking to apparent people, seeing people with faces and bodies, and communicating in that way. Much more happens in this sort of circumstance than any book can ever get near to.

You know, there are so many books. You can take them home and read all these words from great teachers ... That's OK; it's fine. There is some sort of fragrance there. But the most powerful thing of all is to sit with blood and bones and be sitting with that nothingness. That's what is wonderful; that is what I am passionate about. To see that guy – he or she is just like you; he or she is just an ordinary guy. There is nothing extraordinary about him or her. And if there is nothing extraordinary about him, I can be that. I am that – which you are.

If I could, I would give up my life for you to see this. Really! Actually I *have* given up my life – so it's about time that you saw it!

o   o   o

If this room and what we apparently see is what is, how is it that when you stay here and I go outside, my 'what is' is different from yours?

It's not different – it only appears to be so. It is the one appearing and inviting.

How can it be uniquely my invitation if there's no 'me'?

There is no 'you', but uniquely there is a body/mind. That body/mind is unique – that's how consciousness has created it. So everything that arises for that body/mind is uniquely the invitation to discover that there is no separation.

But how can we both be awareness, and yet the phenomena – what we see and experience – are different?

That's because of the diversity of oneness; that's the manifestation of diversity; that's the joy. Everyone in this room sees everything differently, apparently – there isn't actually anyone here, but everything is manifesting differently. That's the richness, that's the fun, that's the joy. In fact, the film that you have out there that you call different isn't actually different. It's the same invitation – it's just a different colour. It only looks different, and in reality it is all simply the one. There is only source appearing.

It's confusing.

I know. It's a mystery. It's a mystery that's wonderful to behold when it's beheld by no one.

We still have to practise – we still have to do something. If you want to take the bus or you want to read or whatever, you have to do something. I had to do something to get here.

Absolutely – you *apparently* had to. If you wanted to run a mile in under four minutes, you would apparently have to practise. If you wanted to get anything, you would have to practise – but there is no one there who chooses that. The one thing that you can never get is your original nature. You will never ever find or get that, because it already is.

All the time there is someone there thinking that they have to do that, all the time there is some idea in that head, in that mind, that traditional practice is what is needed; all the time there is some sort of a link-up with some idea that you have heard from somebody else that this is the way to be – there will always be someone reinforcing the idea of seeking. You are that, you are divine, and so what is there to find?

Fine. I know that. We are all divine.

But knowing this intellectually is nothing. You believe you are Bill who is trying to find something. Be ready to be adventurous. Be ready to chop off all the heads that you have looking at you over the fence telling you how you should be. Be ready to drop all of it.

You know traditions talk about freedom, but this is the freedom - not something written on paper. Forget Buddha – chop Buddha's head off.

They say, if you find Buddha on the road, kill him.

Absolutely. And Buddha – or Buddhism – is apparently on the road telling you that you need to meditate, you need to have right mindfulness, wise action. Chop off its head and rest in the arms of the beloved.

Well, it is difficult because you don't know where you are going.

Nothing is going anywhere. Give up knowing where you are going. If you want to be safe, you are in the wrong place.

You will never be safe anyway. Either way, you will never be safe.

There is only one safe place, there is only one constant safe place, and that is in the arms of the beloved. You are actually always safe; you are always held. It doesn't matter what happens with you in this life you think you are leading – you are actually always held. You can never leave the beloved; you *are* the beloved. Let go of trying to know and just relax into what is.

It seems to help me to get curious about who I am, to inquire. So if I find myself suffering then I might inquire 'Who am I?' Or if my body hurts, I might inquire 'What is this body? Do I own it or do I not own it?'

OK, if that is how it is for that body/mind, that's how it is. But it's very interesting that you're sitting in this room hearing that

225

you don't have to do anything! That's happening in the world now, in this apparent world. The message that's being communicated now is, in certain places, very direct. It's a very direct message, and somewhere people are ready to hear that very direct message.

So walk out of here and practise and be curious, if that is how it's going to be for you. But also be open to the possibility that walking up the corridor is it. Just that. It's the tendency of the mind to think 'When I've gone out of here I'm going to meditate and that's the most important part of the day'. Walking up that path, up that road, out into the open, is that which is arising in present awareness, and there is nothing that needs to be 'done' about that. It is what it is – end of story … end of seeking.

o   o   o

When you were talking about everything can only be as it is because there's nobody to make any decisions or nobody to choose anything different, it struck me very strongly that when that's clearly seen, there is an awful lot of mind-stuff that obviously becomes irrelevant. Because in the very idea of choosing, there's the idea of right and wrong, and me doing better or worse, someone else not doing it right … And it would seem to me that, when it is clearly seen, there's a simplifying in the mind/ body, because any thought or resistance to what is, is clearly ridiculous. So can you confirm if it's true in your experience that the mind becomes simpler?

Oh yes, absolutely, because this is a totally revolutionary and yet fundamentally the natural way of seeing reality. It is what reality is.

Our conditioning is to believe that somehow I'm not quite right and the world isn't quite right and we've got to do something about changing all of that. That's the whole conditioning, that everything has to change and be better and I have to be better.

And it's revolutionary to come to see that actually nothing's happening at all; nothing has ever changed; it is all the same image; it's just different colours. There's nowhere to go and nothing to do. There's no possibility of anywhere to go, because there's no one who can go anywhere. And there's nowhere to go because this is the paradise; this is always, constantly, the paradise.

It's a revolutionary realisation which is beyond time and space and yet embraces them totally. It's incredibly simple, and all the ideas we have, the concepts we have about how we should be and what enlightenment is, simply fall away.

Yes, so I see just a great simplifying. And still you mentioned that even after awakening there's a momentum to the way the mind works (that's the way I would put it), but you know that it's not you, this mind-stuff. Anger could arise, but as long as you are clearly seeing that there's no one there to be angry, then for an awakened person that kind of just falls away like smoke, because there's no grabbing at it and identifying with it.

So in your experience, would you say that there is still a momentum as it were of ridiculous stuff, resisting what is? You know better, but the momentum is still there … you see it, it goes away, it comes back, and that keeps happening. Does it dissipate with time and become less and less, this momentum you can see through?

Yes, it does, in what seems like time. Everything becomes more harmonious and everything slows down. All that anxiety, all that angst and huge positive and negative energy flattens out. 'I will level the mountains and raise the valleys', Christ said. Awakening is that all of those extremes reduce and reduce and reduce. They can't live in that light. Anger can arise, but it can't stay in that light. There's no one any longer who has any hooks in it, has any interest in it. So it can't live in that sort of light.

o   o   o

You've alluded to the idea that there's no such thing as space. Could you talk about that a little bit?

Just as time is a concept, a thought-form, so is space a thought-form. I don't know whether you know but recently scientists have discovered that space is actually a structure rather like molecules. Space simply is a representation, as is everything else that is manifested. It's simply a representation of silence or stillness. The reality is that there is no space between this and that. There is no separation; there is nothing between this and that. Both arise in stillness -both are one in stillness – both are stillness appearing.

Of course, it's the same with time. Time is only a concept – most people understand that already. If we think of the past, we think of it in this. If we anticipate the future, we only ever anticipate it in this. And in three years' time, we still only anticipate the future in this. There is only ever this. Time is an appearance in the drama of the search for that which is beyond.

That's why one comes to see that nothing's happening. Nothing's ever happened – it only appears to have happened; things appear to have happened. All there is is this.

I'm not going to say, 'All there is is now'. There is no 'now', because 'now' implies a 'then'. There is no moment – this has nothing to do with living in the moment. There's no one to live and there's no moment. There's only this.

This reality that emanates, this manifestation, is only being. It's pure being and it seems to have motion. It's actually one image, but the mind puts one image together with the next one, with the next one, and thinks it's a story. It's simply being manifesting. And its only meaning is the invitation. It's like a hologram.

In these sorts of meetings, people come here with concepts about who they are and what enlightenment is, and it's possible that those concepts will be destroyed completely. So it is also possible that one is left with absolutely nothing. And in being left with absolutely nothing – without hope, with nothing – then one suddenly sees this. Just this. And this is the timelessness; this is the timeless wonder of being.

The seeker is always denying God. The seeker is always denying the liberation, the being, that is present. Because the seeker is always looking over there for what already is. So just drop seeking and be the finder, and you don't have to look very far. You don't have to look anywhere.

o o o

I understand intellectually that it's necessary for the belief system in a separate self-existence to drop away for awakening to arise. On the other hand, the thing that seems to cling the strongest – or manifest as the most personal – is the fear, the fear of letting go, or the fear of psychological death. Can you talk about that a little bit?

It doesn't have to happen. In a way, the mind still looks for a process in time. It says, 'Even Tony Parsons says the seeker has to drop away and the cloud has to evaporate for the sun to be there'. Immediately the mind turns that into something that is a process that has to happen; and until that happens, awakening cannot be there. The mind is always making up a list of things – 'Two or three steps have to happen before this takes place'.

Actually, nothing has to happen at all. And in some way or other the mind is tricking the consciousness by saying, 'Oh well, this has to happen, and therefore we have to set up some sort of fear about that, in order to avoid it happening'. There's always some way or other in which the mind will create an issue or a problem around awakening, because it doesn't comprehend awakening. What it does see is that when awakening happens it will no longer be on the throne.

So don't hang on to the idea that steps have to take place. If there is fear, then that's the invitation. The invitation is through the senses – not the story about awakening, but the feeling in the body of fear is the invitation. What is it that sees fear?

That's the genius of the ego, I guess, in a sense doing its work.

Yes, the guru mind, as I call it; the mind that will convince you that it will take you there, it will do everything. It's such a brilliant thing, the mind. It will convince you it will take you there – but it's always *going* to take you there. It never happens – it's always going to happen tomorrow.

o   o   o

Why do we need to relearn or remember, if we already know?

We don't need to relearn – we are already that. Whilst there is a sense of being a separate individual, then there is a sense that there is something to learn. All you're really learning actually is that there is nothing to learn. But why not? It's a good game.

Could you tell me again about how I see everything as the invitation, how this apparent self sees everything as the invitation?

You can't do that; you, as an individual, can't do that. We're speaking here to a wisdom that's deeper than the individual. And that wisdom can see the wonder of this constant invitation, which is timelessness.

o   o   o

Given that life is often expressed in a spiritual metaphor as being like a film, why are we experiencing it one frame at a time rather than being able to see it all?

You are seeing all; you are seeing the beloved. This is all there is. That's all that's needed to be seen. I don't need to see what's going on in Africa. This is it. There isn't an Africa – this is all that is.

Is every particle, every object, simultaneously in a state of apparent separation and reunion?

Yes and no. It's as though everything arises in that. Nothing can be except that that is. In the game of separation, there is a belief that what is seen is the real world. But what is being seen from that body/mind is a separate manifestation; that's the unreal world. When awakening arises or is seen (by no one), when the whole sense of 'me' drops away, then what is seen is real. The real world is simply unconditional love manifesting as this. One is no longer looking at a wall – one is looking at unconditional love, wall-ing.

So everything, the objects, can be an apparent separation and can also simultaneously be an invitation?

Yes, it always is. It always is. The very nature of the separation and the disquiet that's felt here is the invitation or, if you like, the grace. You are in a way being literal about it. The wall is saying, 'You are disquieted because you feel separate from me, but you aren't. See that you are me, I am you'. Of course, once the invitation is taken up, then there's no invitation. I don't live in invitation because there's no one here who needs an invitation. In fact, there is no one here who needs anything. There is simply no separate entity.

o   o   o

You mentioned that there were these people who just became awakened. Who's there to decide who's awakened and not awakened?

Firstly, no one becomes awakened – no person. There's nobody. There is no one. There is no will; there is no God or God's will. There is no such thing as choice anywhere – anywhere at all. The whole idea of choice or will – which is totally a construct of the mind – implies a motive, implies that there's something going somewhere. There isn't anything going anywhere. Choice and will are as much appearances as karma or rebirth or reincarnation. It's simply an idea made up through the mind which maintains the apparent continuance of the drama of the search.

I suppose that one reason that there's no choice is that the supposed person is really this collection of thoughts, memories and so on and so on, which inherently does not have a life and, because of the conditioning, really doesn't have a choice. Is that it?

In the end, actually, it is that there is no one. There is no fixed constant thing which is a 'me'. There never has been anyone, ever, therefore – obviously – there never has been choice. It isn't that there's no choice – it is that there's no one. There's never been anyone.

And that's really the appropriate understanding.

Yes, in the end – except that it's beyond understanding. It's something that can't be described. There is no one here, but I don't understand that. There's no one to understand it anymore. At one time, yes, I did understand the construct, but that was meaningless in a way. It was only something that I knew or heard. 'There is no one here', I said to myself, I said to me. And then I tried to experience not being me … It's like a dog chasing its tail.

o   o   o

I'd like to ask you if you and other awakened people (people, at least, as it appears to me) live continually in this presence or this awareness. Can you speak about that?

First of all, there is no such thing as an awakened person; that's a contradiction in terms. Secondly, there is no one to *do* anything at any level – doing simply appears as doing in the manifestation. So let's say there is just being and 'me'-ing. Liberation has no connection with the concept of *permanent* being, because there is no such thing. If those so-called enlightened people were honest, they would probably say to you that they are mainly in being. There can still be a contraction into 'me'-ing, but the final liberation is that anything is accepted and everything is accepted; nothing is denied. So both are now seen as one.

It is important to see that the question arises from the mind's linear viewpoint which imagines enlightenment as a state similar to good health. Once the perception of oneness has been fully embodied, then everything arises and is seen as the celebration.

You're not in continual surrender?

Liberation is not about someone being in something. There isn't anyone here. Being is in the main the case, but 'me'-ing also can be the case. And both are one.

You seem to be continually aware that you're not there.

That's a contradiction of the mind. I'm not continually aware that I'm not here. There is no one here. There is being, but contraction can happen. It happens within the perception of the whole. Anything can happen because this is liberation. This is life being life.

And I think we have got to be very clear about something else – I am not an individual; I'm not someone or something which has total wisdom and total freedom and therefore cannot possibly experience any sort of anger whatever. I am this – I am all that is! And in that 'all that is' there can be anger, pride, lust … All of that arises in this. It has to be like that.

Liberation includes the total acceptance of all that is. Nothing is denied. Anger arises in this and anger arises in that, and lust arises in this and lust arises in that. That's the manifestation, that's the divine expression. All of it is the divine expression. There's nothing wrong with it. It's the game, it's the celebration – that whole richness is the celebration of this manifestation. It is all the divine expression, which is totally beyond the idea of right or wrong, better or worse, or something becoming something else. That is the game of the mind.

This whole idea we have that once awakening happens somehow you're in a fixed state of blissful goodness comes out of a deep ignorance. And anyway, being in a fixed state of blissful goodness would simply be being in another prison.

o   o   o

I love the game of having somebody sitting there and me sitting here, knowing he's the teacher and I'm the disciple. There's got to be something different between me and you—otherwise you wouldn't be there and I wouldn't be here. That's the way I feel. I think, 'He has to be able to accept everything while I don't'. Is that true?

Let's catch it there. I don't accept anything at all. The difference is that there is no one, so there is nothing to accept or not accept. What you describe is still a dream, the hypnotic dream of someone being there who really should accept everything because that guy up on the stage does—and that's a misconception. There's no one here. So there's nothing to accept or not accept. The only difference between you and me is that I have lost everything; you still own the belief that you are someone.

But there is somebody here who doesn't accept.

So you believe. That's a belief—it's a wisp of smoke, and yet it's very powerfully held there. There's no one there, there's no one standing there. There's only a belief that there is. There's an investment in that—you come to these places and you sit in that seat with an investment in the idea that there's someone sitting there who hasn't got what this guy's got.

I'll tell you the difference—it's me who hasn't got anything. Really—I don't have anything. That's the difference—you have

234

something. You're a rich man – you have 'you' to start with, and you have much knowledge about who you think you are and what should be done about that.

One thing you said is that, in this apparent non-person, anything can arise at any time. But I'm assuming that individuality or your identification with individuality no longer is a possibility? You would no longer think once again that you're Tony Parsons? You know what I mean? Once this happens, this transition is permanent?

For no one, yes, it is. It's utter clarity. There isn't any belief there's nothing. I'm not going to ask any questions any more there's nothing to ask. There's no one to ask.

How do you know that?

I don't – I *am* that. I am the source of all that is.

You mentioned that anything can happen – everything arises and goes away – and contraction can happen, expansion can happen, whatever. The understanding I've always had is that once there is that shift where the sense of individuality drops away permanently, there's a constant continuum of awareness and wakefulness that never goes away. The continuum is there, whatever the seeming world around you; whether your emotions or your feelings contract or expand; or you feel depressed; you feel angry; you feel happy. Underneath all that, whether you're in deep sleep or you're waking, there's a continuum of awareness that's always lively and awake, not involved, just being.

Yes, that is so. But you see, that's how it is here also. It's just not seen that that's how it is. Everybody who's sitting here is having feelings and thoughts going on, but behind that is stillness, utter stillness.

You must feel it right now. You must feel that vertical column of stillness, which is simply sitting there seeing this. It's so simple, it's so utterly there, it's so there now. This silence, this being, is shouting louder than anything else in this room. At the same time it is also all that is arising.

o   o   o

Give me your perspective on two primary issues which come up for me quite often – fear, and external pressures, meaning global, society, individual, all-inclusive …

Separation apparently happens for a very young child when suddenly no longer is the mother just another energy that is himself or herself, but it becomes a mother – a person out there, who calls him or her Peter or Mary. That first moment of suddenly coming to believe 'I am an individual – I'm on my own here' raises the most colossal fear. Colossal fear comes from that sense of being in an alien world, the sense of being separate.

Until separation evaporates there is fear. Of course, the strange joke is that the fear that we feel is the beloved; the fear that we feel is the invitation. There has to be fear because, of course, the fear really is the beloved.

The fear – which is a feeling in here – is the aliveness. The story is bullshit. The story – 'Am I going bankrupt?' or 'Does she love me anymore?' – is just information. The fear is just fear. And the fear is saying, 'Come home'.

So I feel that what you call external pressure is simply another tool that's used to create fear. And actually, of course, there isn't anything external; there is nothing external. Everything arises in this – there is nothing out there. And everything that arises is absolutely exquisitely uniquely there as the invitation for this.

You look at your friends and your friends seem to have slightly different problems to yours, and you see their problems far better than they ever do. But actually that is because their apparent problems are uniquely theirs, and their problems will never be any good for you, they'll never work for you – they're uniquely their invitation and yours are uniquely your invitation. It's just genius, absolute genius.

I don't get the sense that it happens now with you (the no-you of you) but in the beginning, when you were starting to experience your awakening, did the world become an unbearable place for you? The world has become an unbearable place for me in many ways.

My sense, as I've said before, is that as long as there's still separation, then 'the world' is uncomfortable anyway. I mean, to a certain extent some people seem to be able to handle it better than other people. But for most people the sense of the world is disturbing because of this sense of separation. Everything can be a subtle threat, for some people more than others.

o o o

Another thought comes to mind and that is this issue which various traditions include and which Ramana Maharshi spoke of -stilling the mind, being quiet. The identification with the person, with the mind, does take up time and energy ... At one point, a number of years ago, I set about stilling the mind (really just by force of will, at that time) and I became very close to psychotic. And the experience of a still mind is quite awful; it's as barren as barren can be. You really don't want that.

At the present time the stillness comes and goes constantly and thoughts come up within the stillness, but I think there is a left-over problem with this stillness in that a casualty has been not engaging in the intimacy. In a way that's a defence, probably.

Oh absolutely, but it's not a permanent casualty?

No.

I have to say that, as far as I'm concerned, there is no question that the mind can ever be stilled. What I do think happens is a disassociation. It is a fairly rare thing, but it's something that can be brought about by someone who seems to have a very powerful determination. Disassociation seems to be the stilling of the mind, and what one is moving into is something barren, because it's a disassociation from life.

But as far as I'm concerned, the idea of the mind being stilled is a contradiction, and I'm wondering whether it was something else that was actually happening. The mind can only be the mind there cannot be a still mind. I don't need to still my mind – I am stillness, and the mind can be the mind in that.

I feel there's a misconception about this idea of stilling the mind. I am the stillness and, in that, the mind can arise. The mind is only a collection of thoughts – it is stillness moving – and its function is to divide. It is in constant activity because it lives only in time. It is the tool that generates the appearance of the drama. I am the stillness which sees the thoughts arising and falling away.

The traditional teachings which recommend meditation, stilling the mind, killing the ego, are nothing more than a conversation in the mind between an artificial spiritual ego and an artificial ordinary ego. It is pure dualism.

o   o   o

It's very clear in this moment that there is nobody here. There is a seeing that goes this way and that way and there is nobody in here. And this happened in spite of me; I had nothing to do with this. It seems like with exposure to Tony Parsons and others, this seeing just happens. Anything that I've ever tried to do to come into this has taken me further away from it, apparently.

And it seems like there are times where this is more apparent than others; there are times when there is more awakeness than others. Like now, it's so clear that there is nobody here ...

I suppose – if there is a question here – it is, would you say that for the people whom you've seen who have this awakening happening, does there seem to be an establishment or an establishing into nothing?

Yes, absolutely. I mean, there is still a shift in perception that happens, there is a moment when suddenly the whole perception changes – but certainly, before that and after that, there is an establishment of being. In fact, really what's happening is that the 'me'-ing is falling away and the being becomes more apparent.

o   o   o

I just want to say that it's been a pleasure listening to you on Friday and Saturday, and it seems even deeper today; that's what it seems like.

What apparently happens is that there's nothing here and your wisdom is seeing its own source. It's seeing its own nothingness, it's seeing what it is. All that's happening here is that you are talking to you, you are communicating with you. Nothing is seeing its own nothingness.

Where does the storyline come from? Is it all just mind-made stuff that we need to drop, or is there some meaning behind it, in terms of the story of our life and the choices we made leading to here and there? Is that what you're referring to as our storyline?

It's the dream, the dream that source manifests through the mind to create an apparent story which is linear; which is apparently taking the apparent person along a line, along a journey, toward somewhere. It's all a total appearance from source, and the whole thing is a total parable, a metaphor.

We're so convinced that we've lived for thirty years, and this happened and that happened … It's so convincing that we totally believe that we are individuals living in a life story. It's meaningless. All of it is meaningless – except that every part of it is the invitation to see that we are the source.

So we really have no choices at all.

There isn't anyone there.

The apparent self has no choices at all.

The self is only an appearance together with apparent choice. The self cannot choose therefore to bring about its own dissolution, and neither does it need to.

○ ○ ○

You made it clear that at some point – and I don't know if this is in all cases or just generally – there's a very definite shift in perception. What is that event, what happens in that shift? You can't perceive reality, it's not a perception – it's knowing, it's a dawning. What is the characteristic of that particular event that shifts?

Let's call it an apparent happening – it is a dropping of the seeker, the falling away of the 'me' who is trying to get something. Thereafter what is perceived by no one is the natural reality.

It seems there is always, in the stories about it, some noticeable shift that takes place, although depending where you are, it might be more or less radical.

It doesn't have to be a very dramatic event that people record. I generally say, 'Don't look for the great dramatic happening', because these days there's so much awareness surrounding people; there are so many people who know this, who already are open to this.

There's a guy, Roger, who lives in London; for him, it was like that. Before he started coming to my talks, and while he was coming to my talks, he was more and more opened to this – 'There is no one'. It was just there. And he wasn't asking any questions. Then he came to one of the retreats and the final awakening happened. But the final awakening was not a big event – it wasn't 'WOW!' – it was more like 'Wow'.

He came to me one morning and simply said, 'That's it'. But he did report that there was seemingly a moment when there was Roger still somewhere there and then, on that morning, suddenly there was a shift. That's the nearest I can get.

o   o   o

The 'me' has just been dissolving this weekend – it really hasn't been getting off the ground. It sort of rolls around and it tries to get up, but it can't do it, it keeps dissolving. And it's exhausting, the 'me'. I think it's pent-up fears and that sort of thing which create the 'me' ... It's exhausting.

It is exhausted, because it's been spending twenty-five or thirty years continuously constructing 'me'. Every morning it constructs 'me' and it has to keep 'me' together. It really wears you out.

For many people there are two things that happen, and one is there is a tremendous relief; there's a huge relief. For people who have really been at it, when they suddenly hear that all of that was not necessary, there is somehow 'Ahhh!' Secondly, there can be great exhaustion for a while.

It is letting go into the beloved. The beloved invites, and the beloved invites through all the senses and feelings. The idea of the senses is to come home through them – that's what they are there for; that's the aliveness; that's the way it is; that's the connection to aliveness. And the beloved is in that aliveness – in whatever is sensed, heard, tasted, and in whatever is cognised.

Thoughts can arise – they are the beloved, they are the beloved thinking. There's nothing wrong with thinking – thinking anything is the beloved thinking anything. And there is that which sees that arising.

You know religious traditions talk about that illusory being/self getting stronger through the fulfilment of the senses?

241

Any religious ideas or traditional Eastern ideas about awareness or awakening come mainly from deep rejection of aliveness, because they are the mind's re-interpretation in words of that which is beyond the heart and mind of man.

What is can't be in the scriptures; this has nothing to do with the scriptures. The beloved has no interest in the scriptures or the traditions – they're just words written on paper. That's the mind, that's all the mind. The beloved is in the alive, the beloved is in this – immediately in the timeless wonder of this. And the difficulty that the mind has with this is that it is immediate, and it brings about the death of the self. That's what's frightening about it.

When you're in the desert and what you experience through your senses is conditioned by this sensitivity and the intensity of being in the desert ... how do you experience the beloved through the senses when everything that the senses bring becomes so unbearable and overwhelming?

One never experiences the beloved – there is only being the beloved. But everything that manifests is the beloved, the oneness, the absolute, or whatever you wish to call it. Whatever arises, and however unbearable it may seem, it is the invitation to dissolve into the unknowing.

o o o

These dialogues often seem to include deep concepts which are addressing the complexity of the mind, but in the end only point to the utter simplicity and wonder of what is.

As you read these words there is a knowing which embraces this happening. It has always been so ... when you took your first breath, saw your first day, when you eat, sleep, run or walk, drink tea or peel potatoes ... there it is ... timeless being. Through all the struggles, the apparent failures and successes, within all the adventures that seem to be the story of your life there is the one constant that never comes and never goes away it is being.

This book speaks only of that and reminds us of a fragrance, the stillness and silence that is home. This is all there is.

Meetings and residentials with Tony Parsons
take place regularly in the UK and internationally.

For details, visit the website at:
www.theopensecret.com